RISING STARS
Mathematics

Year 1

Concept developed by

Cherri Moseley and Caroline Clissold

Year 1 Author Team

Linda Glithro, Emma Low,
Cherri Moseley

Pupil Textbook

The Publishers would like to thank the following for permission to reproduce copyright material.

Photo credits
Pages 10-11: feet; door; bus – Shutterstock; page 25: birds; child eating breakfast; child on slide – Shutterstock; pages 34-5: beach huts; mosaic; building – Shutterstock; crazy paving: iStock; page 47: hour glass; breakfast; table and jug – Shutterstock; pages 58-9: eggbox; drawers; bananas; domino – Shutterstock; page 70-1: shop – Shutterstock; market – iStock; page 81: penny – Shutterstock; page 83: drain; lockers – Shutterstock; page 91: space station – NASA; pages 92-3: swimming pool; child in over-sized clothes; cat on wall; men fishing: Shutterstock; page 103: baby – Shutterstock; baby elephant – Wikipedia Commons; pages 104-5: calendar; clock; ruler; tape measure; thermometer – Shutterstock; page 113: clock on Westminster Abbey – Shutterstock; pages 114-15: robot; shelves; warehouse; bracelet – Shutterstock; page 123: Earth from space – Shutterstock; pages 124-5: hands; egg cups – Shutterstock; pages 138-9: market – iStock; slicer; classroom – Shutterstock; pages 148-9: twin girls; clock – Shutterstock; page 159: folding paper – Shutterstock; pages 160-1: apples; road signs; stairs; roundabout; clock - Shutterstock

Acknowledgements
The reasoning skills on page 8 are based on John Mason's work on mathematical powers.
See Mason, J. and Johnston-Wilder, S. (Eds.) (2004). Learners powers. *Fundamental constructs in Mathematics Education*. London: Routledge Falmer. 115-142.

Every effort has been made to trace all copyright holders, but if any have been inadvertently overlooked, the Publishers will be pleased to make the necessary arrangements at the first opportunity.
Although every effort has been made to ensure that website addresses are correct at time of going to press, Rising Stars cannot be held responsible for the content of any website mentioned in this book. It is sometimes possible to find a relocated web page by typing in the address of the home page for a website in the URL window of your browser.

Hachette UK's policy is to use papers that are natural, renewable and recyclable products and made from wood grown in sustainable forests. The logging and manufacturing processes are expected to conform to the environmental regulations of the country of origin.

ISBN: 978 1 78339 522 4
Text, design and layout © Rising Stars UK Ltd 2015
First published in 2015 by
Rising Stars UK Ltd, part of Hodder Education,
An Hachette UK Company
Carmelite House
50 Victoria Embankment
London EC4Y 0DZ
www.risingstars-uk.com
Authors: Caroline Clissold, Linda Glithro, Steph King

Programme consultants: Cherri Moseley, Caroline Clissold, Paul Broadbent
Publishers: Fiona Lazenby and Alexandra Riley
Editorial: Kate Baxter, Jane Carr, Sarah Chappelow, Jan Fisher, Lucy Hyde, Lynette James, Shannon Keenlyside, Jackie Mace, Jane Morgan, Christine Vaughan
Project manager: Sue Walton
Series and character design: Steve Evans
Illustrations by Steve Evans

Cover design: Steve Evans and Words & Pictures
Printed by Liberduplex, Barcelona
A catalogue record for this title is available from the British Library.

Contents

Introduction

Hello, I'm Jen. Welcome to *Rising Stars Mathematics!*

Look at the pictures at the beginning of the unit. Think about the mathematics you can see in the world around you.

Talk about the questions with your friends. Do you agree on the answers?

Read what Amy and Theo say. Can you spot if they have made a mistake?

Read the text and look at the diagrams to learn new maths skills. Your teacher will explain them.

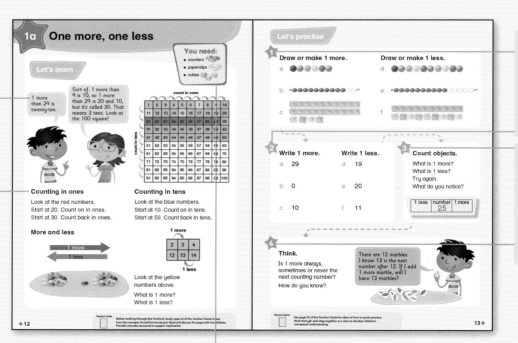

Do these activities to practise what you have learnt. Write the answers in your exercise book.

These questions will help you explore and investigate maths. You will need to think about them carefully.

Use these items to help you. Make sure you have everything you need.

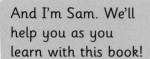

And I'm Sam. We'll help you as you learn with this book!

Play the game at the end of the unit to practise what you have learnt.

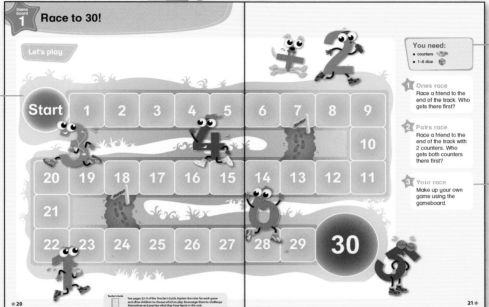

Game board 1 — Race to 30!

Let's play

Start 1 2 3 4 5 6 7 8 9 10 11 12 13 14 15 16 17 18 19 20 21 22 23 24 25 26 27 28 29 **30**

★20

Teacher's Guide: See pages 32–3 of the Teacher's Guide. Explain the rules for each game and allow children to choose which to play. Encourage them to challenge themselves and practise what they have learnt in the unit.

21★

You need:
- counters
- 1–6 dice

Make sure you have everything you need.

1 Ones race
Race a friend to the end of the track. Who gets there first?

2 Pairs race
Race a friend to the end of the track with 2 counters. Who gets both counters there first?

3 Your race
Make up your own game using the gameboard.

Follow the instructions to use the gameboard in different ways.

Try these activities to check what you have learnt in the unit. Have you understood all the new maths concepts?

Review 1 — And finally ...

Let's review

24   1 more   25

Pick 5 number cards. Find 1 more for each.
Now find 1 less for the same numbers.
What do you notice?

You need:
- number cards (2–49)

2 Roll 2 dice. Make two 2-digit numbers.
Draw or make each number.

14
41

What is the largest number you can make? What is the smallest?

You need:
- two 1–6 dice
- Base 10 apparatus

★22

Teacher's Guide: See pages 34–5 of the Teacher's Guide for guidance on running each task. Observe children to identify those who have mastered concepts and those who require further consolidation.

3 Look at the numbers and pictures. What's wrong?
Change the number or the picture to make them match.

4 1 →

2 4 →

3 7 ↓

You need:
- Base 10 apparatus
- place-value cards (1–40)
- counters
- ten frames

Did you know?

Four

Four is the only number with the same number of letters in the word as its name.

All 2-digit numbers are made up of tens and ones. We have 10 fingers and thumbs. What other tens can you think of?

Find out more about maths by reading these fun facts!

23★

7★

Try these ideas to develop your reasoning skills. Doing this will help you improve your mathematical thinking.

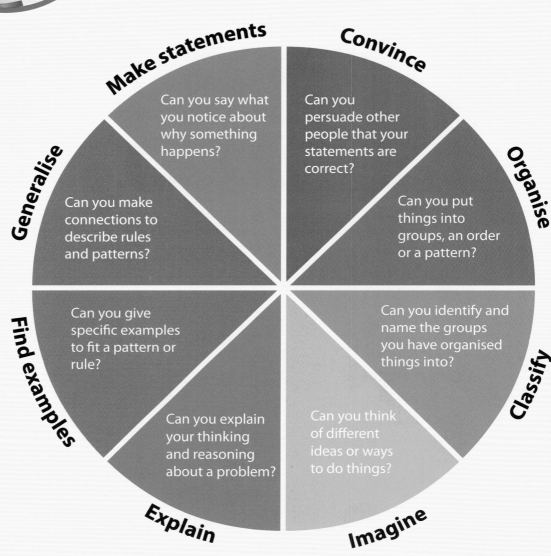

Make statements — Can you say what you notice about why something happens?

Convince — Can you persuade other people that your statements are correct?

Organise — Can you put things into groups, an order or a pattern?

Classify — Can you identify and name the groups you have organised things into?

Imagine — Can you think of different ideas or ways to do things?

Explain — Can you explain your thinking and reasoning about a problem?

Find examples — Can you give specific examples to fit a pattern or rule?

Generalise — Can you make connections to describe rules and patterns?

1 Read the problem carefully.

2 What do you need to find out?

3 What data or information is given in the problem?

4 What data or information do you need to use?

5 Make a plan for what to do.

6 Follow your plan to find the answer.

7 Check your answer. Is it correct? Put your answer into the problem to see if it works with the information given.

8 Evaluate your method. How could you improve it next time?

Numbers everywhere!

What else do I have 10 of?

I wonder where number 28 is?

27

5

5 is a special number. I'm 5!

9 is a special number. That's the bus I catch to go to see granddad.

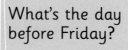

What's the day before Friday?

Birthday! Party!

Friday 3rd October

5 is a special number. I'm 5!

I wonder if she is still the tallest?

Teacher's Guide
Look at the pictures with the children and discuss the questions.
See pages 22–3 of the *Teacher's Guide* for key ideas to draw out.

11 ★

One more, one less

Let's learn

1 more than 29 is twenty-ten.

Sort of. 1 more than 9 is 10, so 1 more than 29 is 20 and 10, but it's called 30. That means 3 tens. Look at the 100 square!

count in ones

1	2	3	4	5	6	7	8	9	10
11	12	13	14	15	16	17	18	19	20
21	22	23	24	25	26	27	28	29	30
31	32	33	34	35	36	37	38	39	40
41	42	43	44	45	46	47	48	49	50
51	52	53	54	55	56	57	58	59	60
61	62	63	64	65	66	67	68	69	70
71	72	73	74	75	76	77	78	79	80
81	82	83	84	85	86	87	88	89	90
91	92	93	94	95	96	97	98	99	100

count in tens

Counting in ones

Look at the red numbers.
Start at 20. Count on in ones.
Start at 30. Count back in ones.

Counting in tens

Look at the blue numbers.
Start at 10. Count on in tens.
Start at 50. Count back in tens.

More and less

1 more
1 less

1 more

2	3	4
12	13	14

1 less

Look at the yellow numbers above.

What is 1 more?
What is 1 less?

1

Draw or make 1 more.

a

b

c

Draw or make 1 less.

d

e

f

2

Write 1 more.

a   29

b   0

c   10

Write 1 less.

d   19

e   20

f   11

3

Count objects.

What is 1 more?
What is 1 less?
Try again.
What do you notice?

1 less	number	1 more
	25	

4

Think.

Is 1 more always, sometimes or never the next counting number?

How do you know?

There are 12 marbles. I know 13 is the next number after 12. If I add 1 more marble, will I have 13 marbles?

Teacher's Guide

See page 25 of the *Teacher's Guide* for ideas of how to guide practice. Work through each step together as a class to develop children's conceptual understanding.

13 ⭐

Tens and ones

You need:
- ten frames
- counters
- place-value cards or counters

Let's learn

Ten

10 is a very important number.

Show 7 on a ten frame. How many empty squares are there?

23 is 2 ones and 3 tens.

That's the wrong way round. 23 is 20 and 3. That's 2 tens for the 20 and 3 ones.

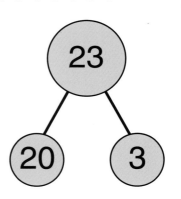

Place value

2-digit numbers are made of tens and ones. Look how to show 23.

20   3

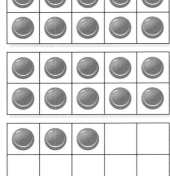

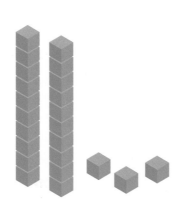

Choose a number. How can you show it?

Teacher's Guide

Before working through the *Textbook*, study page 26 of the *Teacher's Guide* to see how the concepts should be introduced. Read and discuss the page with the children. Provide concrete resources to support exploration.

Let's practise

Write.

Show a number on a ten frame.
Look at the empty squares.
Write the number bond.
Try again.

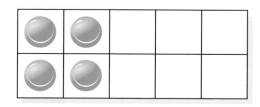

$4 + 6 = 10$

Copy and complete.

a
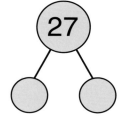

b
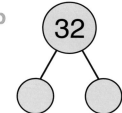

c
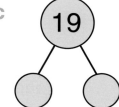

d
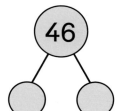

e
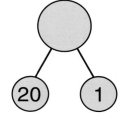

f
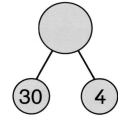

Think.

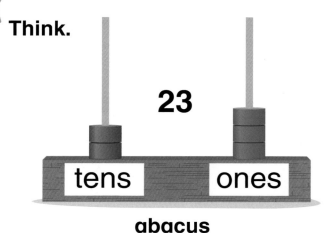

23

tens   ones

abacus

There are 2 rings on the tens spike and 3 rings on the ones spike.

10…20…21…22…23!

What numbers can you make with 5 rings?

Teacher's Guide See page 27 of the *Teacher's Guide* for ideas of how to guide practice.
Work through each step together as a class to develop children's
conceptual understanding.

15

1c Length and height

You need:

- objects to compare
- cubes
- pencil
- scissors

Let's learn

I'm taller than Samantha and Tom, so they must be the same height.

No, they are both shorter than you, but that doesn't mean they are the same height.

Long, longer, longest

 long

longer

longest

How many cubes long is each object?

Tall, taller, tallest

Find 3 objects.

How many cubes tall are they?

Which is the tallest?

tall   taller   tallest

Short, shorter, shortest

Use your objects to show short, shorter and shortest.

What did you change?

short   shorter   shortest

Teacher's Guide

Before working through the *Textbook*, study page 28 of the *Teacher's Guide* to see how the concepts should be introduced. Read and discuss the page with the children. Provide concrete resources to support exploration.

1 Draw.

Draw a big footprint.
Find 3 things that are:

a longer

b shorter

c about the same length

2 Count.

How many cubes long is your big footprint?

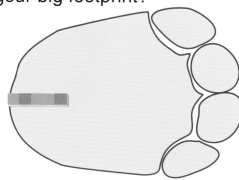

3 Count and compare.

a How long is the shortest snake?

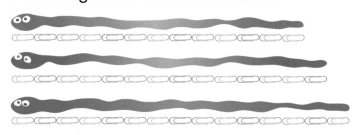

b How tall is the shortest pencil?

c How many beads on the longer string?

4 Think. How many cubes?

a a longer snake

b a shorter snake

c a snake the same length

Teacher's Guide

See page 29 of the *Teacher's Guide* for ideas of how to guide practice. Work through each step together as a class to develop children's conceptual understanding.

17 ★

Let's learn

Today is Wednesday, so yesterday was Thursday!

No, it's Thursday tomorrow. Yesterday was Tuesday.

You need:
- paper and pencil
- scissors
- glue
- counters

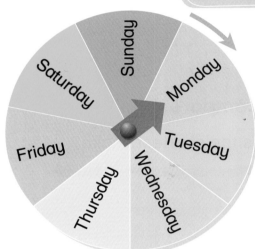

Days of the week

The days of the week always follow the same order. Start from Monday.

Months of the year

The months of the year always follow the same order. Start from January.

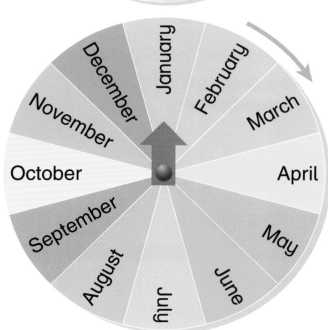

Teacher's Guide

Before working through the *Textbook*, study page 30 of the *Teacher's Guide* to see how the concepts should be introduced. Read and discuss the page with the children. Provide concrete resources to support exploration.

> The day before Wednesday is Tuesday.

> The day after Wednesday is Thursday.

1 Write.

Use the week wheel. Choose a day. Write:

a   the day before

b   the day after

Repeat.

Day before	Today	Day after
Tuesday	Wednesday	Thursday

2 Write.

Order the months from September. What happens in each month?

September
new class

July

December

January

August

April

October

3 Draw and write. Choose:

a   a day of the week

b   a month of the year

March	Thursday
Monday	December
August	Sunday

Use words like:

school	spring	summer
autumn	winter	hot
cold	holiday	birthday

4 Think.

Write a date in numbers and words.

a   Choose a date to write.

b   Write the day before.

c   Write the day after.

Repeat.

September 2014						
SUNDAY	MONDAY	TUESDAY	WEDNESDAY	THURSDAY	FRIDAY	SATURDAY
	1	2	3	4	5	6
7	8	9	10	11	12	13
14	15	16	17	18	19	20
21	22	23	24	25	26	27
28	29	30				

17.09.14

Wednesday 17th September 2014

Teacher's Guide   See page 31 of the *Teacher's Guide* for ideas of how to guide practice. Work through each step together as a class to develop children's conceptual understanding.

19 ★

Race to 30!

Let's play

Start	1	2	3	4	5

20	19	18	17	16	15

Shortcut

21					

22	23	24	25	26	27

Teacher's Guide See pages 32–3 of the *Teacher's Guide*. Explain the rules for each game and allow children to choose which to play. Encourage them to challenge themselves and practise what they have learnt in the unit.

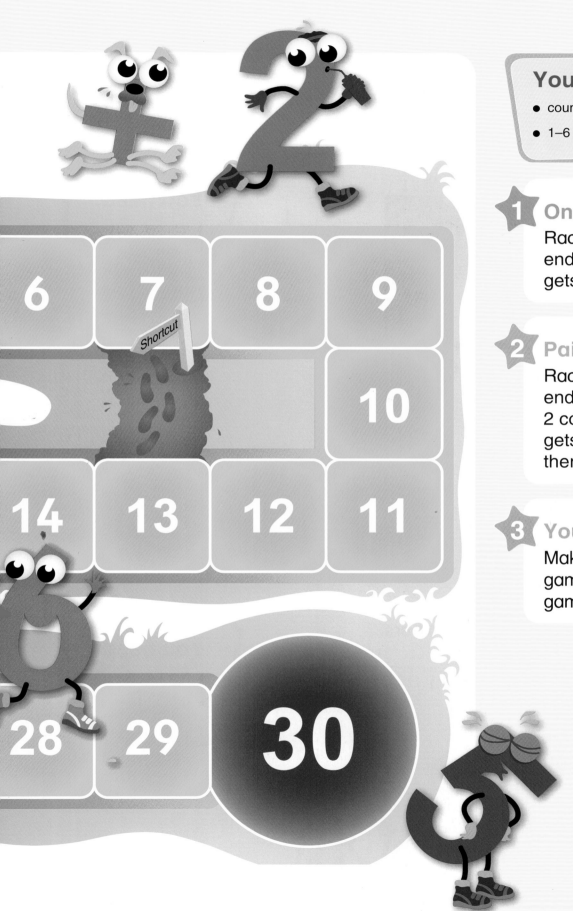

You need:

- counters
- 1–6 dice

1 **Ones race**

Race a friend to the end of the track. Who gets there first?

2 **Pairs race**

Race a friend to the end of the track with 2 counters. Who gets both counters there first?

3 **Your race**

Make up your own game using the gameboard.

And finally ...

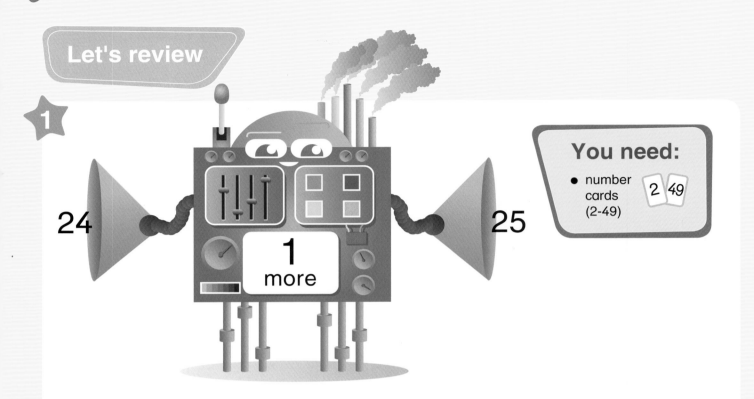

24   1 more   25

You need:
- number cards (2-49)

Pick 5 number cards. Find 1 more for each.

Now find 1 less for the same numbers.

What do you notice?

 Roll 2 dice. Make two 2-digit numbers.

Draw or make each number.

14
41

You need:
- two 1–6 dice
- Base 10 apparatus

What is the largest number you can make? What is the smallest?

Teacher's Guide

 See pages 34–5 of the *Teacher's Guide* for guidance on running each task. Observe children to identify those who have mastered concepts and those who require further consolidation.

3 Look at the numbers and pictures. What's wrong?

Change the number or the picture to make them match.

You need:
- Base 10 apparatus
- place-value cards (1–40)
- counters
- ten frames

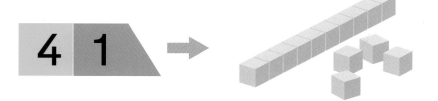

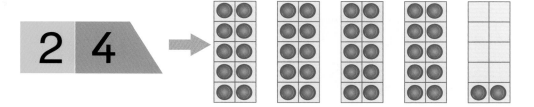

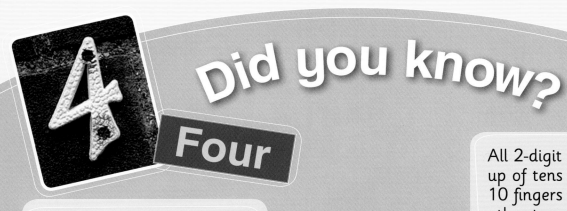

Did you know?

Four

Four is the only number with the same number of letters in the word as its name.

All 2-digit numbers are made up of tens and ones. We have 10 fingers and thumbs. What other tens can you think of?

23

Adding, subtracting and sequencing

Do you think all the birds will fly away?

I wonder what happened next?

What happened before this?

Teacher's Guide
Look at the pictures with the children and discuss the questions.
See pages 36–7 of the *Teacher's Guide* for key ideas to draw out.

25 ⭐

Number stories

You need:
- ten frames
- counters, cubes or other small counting objects

Let's learn

6 add 4 is 10 so 6 take away 4 is 10.

That's not quite right! 6 fingers add 4 fingers makes 10 fingers, so 10 fingers take away 4 fingers takes me back to 6 fingers. 6 fingers take away 4 fingers only leaves 2 fingers!

All about 10

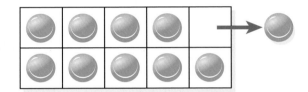

$10 - 0 = 10$

$10 - 1 = 9$

What if 2 counters were moved off the ten frame?

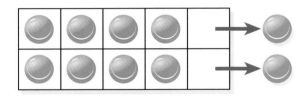

Number story for 7

$7 + 0 = 7$	$7 - 0 = 7$
$6 + 1 = 7$	$7 - 1 = 6$
$5 + 2 = 7$	$7 - 2 = 5$
$4 + 3 = 7$	$7 - 3 = 4$
$3 + 4 = 7$	$7 - 4 = 3$
$2 + 5 = 7$	$7 - 5 = 2$
$1 + 6 = 7$	$7 - 6 = 1$
$0 + 7 = 7$	$7 - 7 = 0$

How are the number statements on the same line linked?

Teacher's Guide

Before working through the *Textbook*, study page 38 of the *Teacher's Guide* to see how the concepts should be introduced. Read and discuss the page with the children. Provide concrete resources to support exploration.

1

Count.

Write all the subtraction bonds for 10.

Start with 10 counters and take away 0, then 1, then 2, and so on.

Always start with 10 and write 10 − =

2

Count.

Make a ten frame into a six frame.

Find all the addition and subtraction number statements for 6.

3

Apply.

12 sheep live in a field.

Every day, a different number of sheep go through a gap in the hedge but they always come back at night.

Write a number statement to show what might have happened in the field each day for a week.

For example, Monday 12 − 5 = 7.

4

Think.

You need 8 counters.

- Player 1 picks up some of the 8 counters while Player 2 has their eyes closed.

- Player 2 works out how many counters Player 1 must have in their hand.

- Check to see if Player 2 is correct.

- Take turns at hiding counters and working out how many counters must be hidden.

Teacher's Guide

See page 39 of the *Teacher's Guide* for ideas of how to guide practice. Work through each step together as a class to develop children's conceptual understanding.

27 ★

Let's learn

My shoes don't feel right since we had PE.

You should have put your socks on before you put your shoes on!

Before and after

Before Sam could eat his sandwich, he had to make it.
After he had eaten his sandwich, there were only crumbs left!

Morning, afternoon and evening

What did Jen do in the **morning**? What did she do **after** school?

Teacher's Guide

Before working through the *Textbook*, study page 40 of the *Teacher's Guide* to see how the concepts should be introduced. Read and discuss the page with the children. Provide concrete resources to support exploration.

Answer these.

Talk about what is happening in the picture.

What happened before this picture? What could happen next, after this picture?

2 Sort.

Draw and label 3 daytime boxes like these.
Sort the words into the correct boxes.

Morning	Afternoon	Evening

Now draw or write 1 more thing in each box.

supper   lunch   after lunch
going to bed
breakfast   before bedtime
waking up   before lunch   afternoon nap
after school   before school

3 Draw.

Draw or write what happened before the picture.

Now draw what might have happened after the picture.

4 Think.

Make a counter snake like this one.
The is first. The is next.
The is after the .
The is after the .

Make and draw this counter snake.
The is first. The is last.
The is next to the .
The is after the .

Work with a partner. Take turns to tell each other how to make a counter snake. Use words like first, before, after, next and last.

Teacher's Guide   See page 41 of the *Teacher's Guide* for ideas of how to guide practice. Work through each step together as a class to develop children's conceptual understanding.

29 ★

Dinosaur pool

Let's play

Teacher's Guide

See pages 42–3 of the *Teacher's Guide*. Explain the rules for each game and allow children to choose which to play. Encourage them to challenge themselves and practise what they have learnt in the unit.

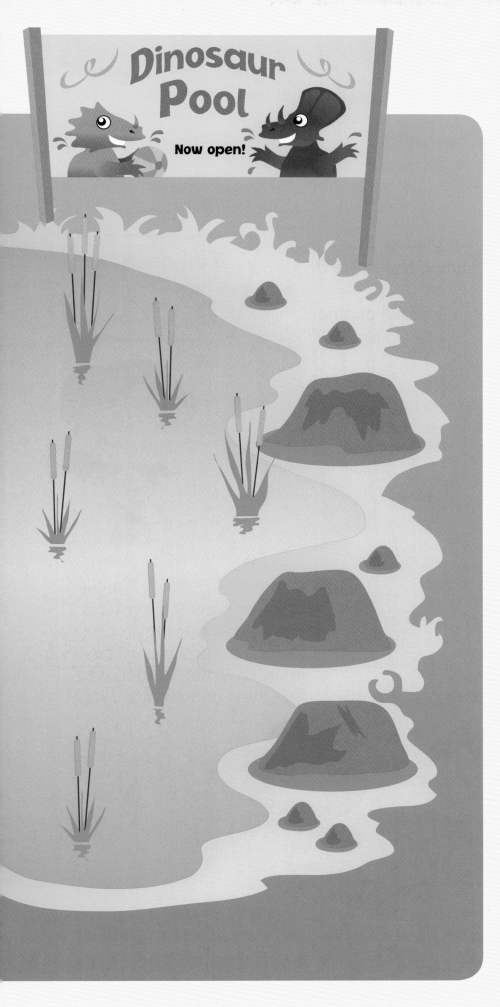

Dinosaur Pool

Now open!

1 Morning swim

Can you get all 8 dinosaurs out of the pool after their morning swim?

2 Afternoon nap

Can you get all 13 dinosaurs into the pool after their afternoon nap?

3 Your game

Make up your own game using the gameboard.

And finally ...

Let's review

1

Shuffle the cards and turn over the top 3 cards.
Can you use the cards and symbols to make a number statement?
If you can, you should be able to make another,
... and another
... and another!
Shuffle the cards and try again with another 3 cards.

You need:

- set of digit cards, (0 to 9, +, − and =)

Sometimes you will not be able to make a number statement, but don't give up too soon!

2

Write or draw 3 things that you did earlier today, **before** this activity. Make sure you record them in the order you did them, starting with what you did first, then next, then last.

Write or draw 3 things that you will do **after** this activity. Make sure you record them in order. What will you do first, next and last?

Teacher's Guide

See pages 44–5 of the *Teacher's Guide* for guidance on running each task. Observe children to identify those who have mastered concepts and those who require further consolidation.

Here are 4 sets of number statements.
Each set of number statements has a different missing number.
Work out the 4 missing numbers.

a   6 + ☐ = 7

   ☐ + 6 = 7

   7 – ☐ = 6

   7 – 6 = ☐

   ☐ = ?

b   ☐ + 2 = 9

   2 + ☐ = 9

   9 – 2 = ☐

   9 – ☐ = 2

   ☐ = ?

c   ☐ – 3 = 9

   ☐ – 9 = 3

   9 + 3 = ☐

   3 + 9 = ☐

   ☐ = ?

d   ☐ = 3 + 5

   ☐ = 5 + 3

   3 = ☐ – 5

   5 = ☐ – 3

   ☐ = ?

Did you know?

There is only 1 of lots and lots of things. There is 1 North Pole, 1 Tower of London, 1 Sahara Desert and only 1 of you. Each of these things is unique.

Words beginning with uni- or mono- usually mean it has only 1 of something. So a unicycle has 1 wheel, a unicorn has 1 horn and a monocle is an eyeglass for 1 eye.

3-D and 2-D shapes

What can you do here?

What shapes can you see?

I wonder how this lovely mosaic was made?

What shapes can you see?

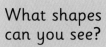

I wonder what shapes are good for building?

Teacher's Guide
Look at the pictures with the children and discuss the questions.
See pages 46–7 of the *Teacher's Guide* for key ideas to draw out.

35 ★

Let's learn

You need:
- 3-D shapes
- boxes
- torch

Cuboids and cubes look the same to me.

They are similar but all the faces of a cube are square. The faces of a cuboid can be rectangles or squares.

Cuboids and cubes

Cuboids have long edges and short edges. Each face can be a rectangle or a square.

The edges on cubes are all the same length. The cube looks the same however you turn it.

More 3-D shapes

A pyramid has faces that are triangles. The triangles meet at a point.

The bottom face of this pyramid is a square.

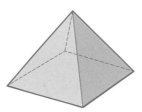

A sphere has a curved surface.

It looks the same however you turn it.

The bottom face of this pyramid is a triangle.

A cylinder has 1 curved surface. It has 2 faces that are circles.

Teacher's Guide

Before working through the *Textbook*, study page 48 of the *Teacher's Guide* to see how the concepts should be introduced. Read and discuss the page with the children. Provide concrete resources to support exploration.

1 Sort.

Sort some 3-D shapes into 2 groups:
- shapes with **curved** edges
- shapes with **straight** edges.

Now sort them in a different way.

2 Compare. Look at these pairs of shapes.

Compare them.

a   b   c   d

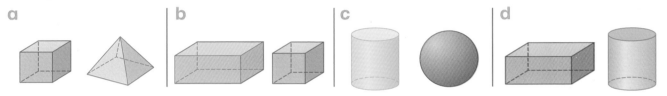

3 Apply. Make a tower of boxes.

Make it as tall as you.

How many boxes did you use?

4 Think.

a   What 3-D shapes could make this shadow?

b   What 3-D shapes could **not** make this shadow?

Teacher's Guide

See page 49 of the *Teacher's Guide* for ideas of how to guide practice. Work through each step together as a class to develop children's conceptual understanding.

37 ⭐

3b 2-D shapes

Let's learn

You need:

- 2-D shapes
- geoboard
- rubber bands
- spotty paper
- geostrips
- split pins

I'm not sure if these are all triangles.

Yes they are! They have 3 sides and triangles always have 3 sides. The sides can be different lengths.

2-D faces on 3-D shapes

The flat faces on 3-D shapes are called 2-D shapes.

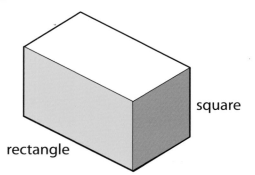

square

rectangle

2-D shapes

Look at some models of 2-D shapes.

A **triangle** has 3 sides.

A **rectangle** has 4 sides. 2 sides are short. 2 sides are long.

A **square** has 4 sides the same length.

A **circle** has a curved side.

Teacher's Guide

Before working through the *Textbook*, study page 50 of the *Teacher's Guide* to see how the concepts should be introduced. Read and discuss the page with the children. Provide concrete resources to support exploration.

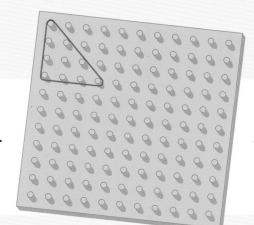

1

Copy and complete.

Make 3 different triangles to fit on a geoboard.
Draw the triangles on
spotty paper.

2

Copy and complete.

Look at the 'shape person' Sam drew using 2-D shapes.
Copy and complete the sentence.
The person is made from ▢ circles, ▢ rectangles
and ▢ squares.
Use models of 2-D shapes to design your own shape person.

3

Apply.

Be a shape detective!
Look for a rectangle in the classroom.
Now look for a bigger rectangle.

Do the same for these shapes: circle square triangle

4

Think.

Use geostrips to make some triangles.
What do you notice about
your triangles?

Teacher's Guide

See page 51 of the *Teacher's Guide* for ideas of how to guide practice.
Work through each step together as a class to develop children's
conceptual understanding.

39 ⭐

Position, direction and movement

Let's learn

Oh, no! I went 10 places to the right but I still didn't reach the treasure!

I expect you went 10 places left! I used to muddle left and right. Let's check what you did.

Talking about position

There are boats on the bottom shelf.
There are cars on the middle shelf.
There are aeroplanes on the top shelf.

The blue toys are on the left.
The red toys are on the right.

The rabbit is inside the hutch.
The dog is outside the hutch.
There is a parrot on top of the hutch.
Can you see what is behind the hutch?

Moving objects

Sam is going up the stairs.

Jen is coming down.

Jen can make the car move forwards and backwards.
She can make it turn to the left and right.

Teacher's Guide

Before working through the *Textbook*, study page 52 of the *Teacher's Guide* to see how the concepts should be introduced. Read and discuss the page with the children. Provide concrete resources to support exploration.

1 Answer these.

Which shape is on the:

a   top row on the right?

b   bottom row on the left?

Where is the:

c   orange cube?

d   green cuboid?

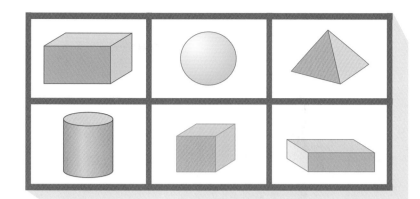

2 Draw.

Draw a picture of Sam in the middle of your paper.

Add:

• a bird **above** Sam

• a tree on the **right** of him

• a large box on the **left** of him

• a cat **inside** the box.

Draw 1 more thing in your picture.

Describe where you have put it.

3 Write.

Write instructions to move the robot along the path.

Start like this: Move up 1 square.

4 Think.

Work with a partner. Write instructions to get from your classroom to somewhere else in school.

Check the number of steps.

Check which way to turn.

Teacher's Guide
See page 53 of the *Teacher's Guide* for ideas of how to guide practice. Work through each step together as a class to develop children's conceptual understanding.

Everyday shapes!

Let's play

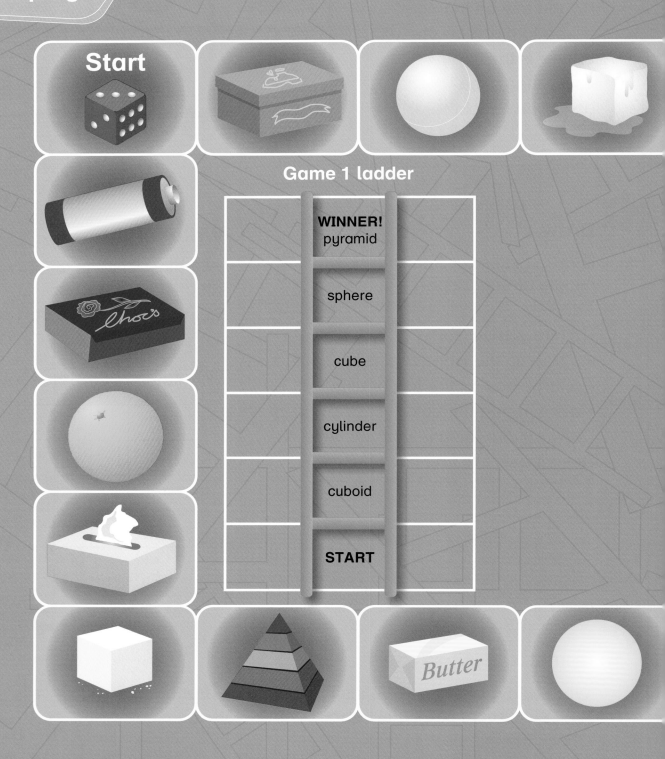

Start

Game 1 ladder

WINNER!
pyramid

sphere

cube

cylinder

cuboid

START

Teacher's Guide

See pages 54–5 of the *Teacher's Guide*. Explain the rules for each game and allow children to choose which to play. Encourage them to challenge themselves and practise what they have learnt in the unit.

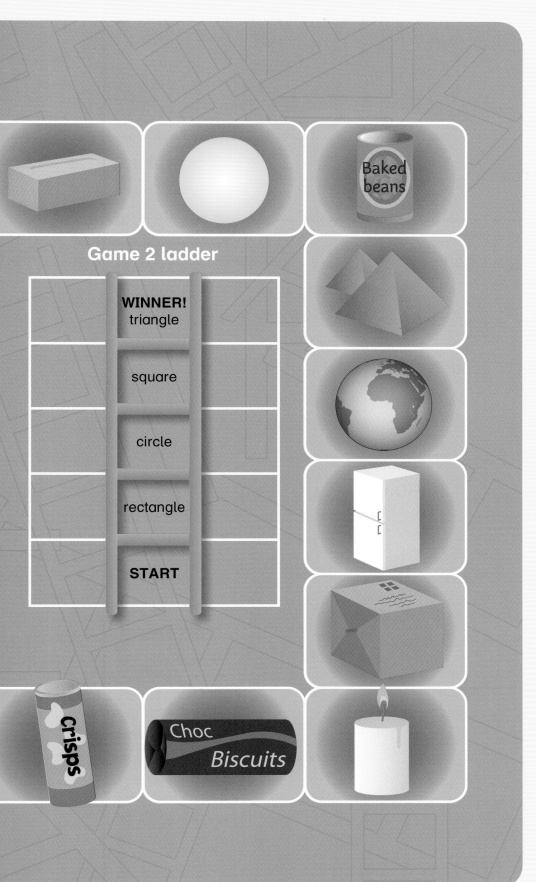

Game 2 ladder

WINNER!
triangle

square

circle

rectangle

START

1 **Climb the ladder!**
Land on 3-D shapes and move up the ladder.

2 **Find the face!**
Find shapes with different faces to move up the ladder.

3 **Your game**
Make up your own game using the gameboard.

43 ★

And finally …

1 Copy the grid.

You need:

- squared paper
- 2-D shapes

Draw these shapes in your grid.

- yellow circle
- small red circle
- blue triangle

- red rectangle
- small yellow rectangle
- green square

Write some sentences to describe the positions of the shapes.
Use the words below.

bottom	right	left	above
below		middle	top

2 Look at your cuboids, cubes and cylinders.
Use them to build a bridge.
Draw your bridge.
Count how many bricks there are
in your bridge.

You need:

- cuboids
- cubes
- cylinders

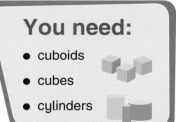

Teacher's Guide

See pages 56–7 of the *Teacher's Guide* for guidance on running each task.
Observe children to identify those who have mastered concepts and those who
require further consolidation.

3 Sam and Jen race their quad bikes to the finish line.

- counters

Describe a path for Sam's red bike. Use direction words.

Watch out for the trees and ponds!

Describe a different path for Jen's blue bike.

Which bike do you think will win?

Did you know?

The ancient Egyptians built stone pyramids. The pyramids are thousands of years old.

There is a modern glass and metal pyramid at the Louvre museum in Paris.

Counting and comparing

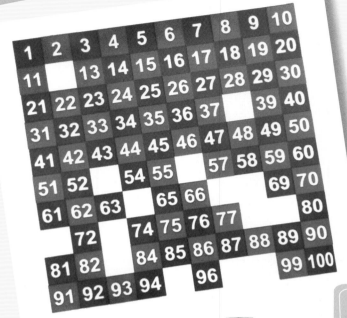

How much longer until the sand has gone?

What time did he have breakfast?

1 glass is full. What about the others?

Teacher's Guide   Look at the pictures with the children and discuss the questions.
See pages 58–9 of the *Teacher's Guide* for key ideas to draw out.

47

Let's learn

You need:

- place-value cards 4 9
- 100 square
- squared paper

Look at the number square. The next door number is 1 more.

Only if it comes *after* the number. If it comes *before* it's 1 less.

1 to 9 again and again

Look at the yellow numbers.
Count from 1 to 9.
Can you see 1 to 9 in another row?

Look at the green numbers.
Count from 12 to 92.
These numbers have 1 ten to 9 tens.
Can you see 1 ten to 9 tens in another column?

row →

1	2	3	4	5	6	7	8	9	10
11	12	13	14	15	16	17	18	19	20
21	22	23	24	25	26	27	28	29	30
31	32	33	34	35	36	37	38	39	40
41	42	43	44	45	46	47	48	49	50
51	52	53	54	55	56	57	58	59	60
61	62	63	64	65	66	67	68	69	70
71	72	73	74	75	76	77	78	79	80
81	82	83	84	85	86	87	88	89	90
91	92	93	94	95	96	97	98	99	100

column

1 more and 1 less than 8

Read these numbers.

68   38   98

Each number has 8 ones. What is 1 more than each number?
Check on the 100 square. Were you right?

What is 1 less than each number?
Check on the 100 square. Were you right?

Teacher's Guide

Before working through the *Textbook*, study page 60 of the *Teacher's Guide* to see how the concepts should be introduced. Read and discuss the page with the children. Provide concrete resources to support exploration.

1 Answer these.

Copy and complete each row and column.

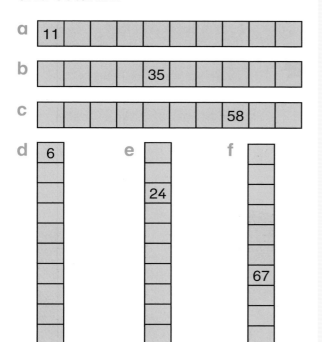

a | 11 | | | | | | | | | |

b | | | | 35 | | | | | | |

c | | | | | | | 58 | | |

d | 6 |

e | | 24 |

f | | | | 67 |

2 Answer these.

Write 1 more than each number. Use the 100 square or place-value cards to help.

a 26   b 36   c 46

d 56   e ?6

What do you notice?

Write 1 less than each number.

f 43   g 53   h 63

i 73   j ?3

What do you notice?

3 Apply.

Make a 100 square.
Use 10 strips of squared paper.
Have 10 squares on each strip.
Will your strips be rows or columns?
Write the numbers.

4 Think.

The 1 to 9 pattern isn't just in rows and columns in the 100 square, it's everywhere!

Is he right? Can you find some more 1 to 9 patterns in the 100 square? Can you explain why the pattern happens?

Teacher's Guide
See page 61 of the *Teacher's Guide* for ideas of how to guide practice. Work through each step together as a class to develop children's conceptual understanding.

49

Let's learn

Faster means more!

Not always. It means doing the same thing in less time. If I walk faster than you, I get there first.

Faster, slower

How far can you count?

If you count faster, you will say more numbers and reach a larger number.

If you count slower, you will say fewer numbers and reach a smaller number.

Earlier, later

7 o'clock is earlier than 8 o'clock.   9 o'clock is later than 8 o'clock.

Teacher's Guide

Before working through the *Textbook*, study page 62 of the *Teacher's Guide* to see how the concepts should be introduced. Read and discuss the page with the children. Provide concrete resources to support exploration.

1

Count. Do something for 1 minute.

Bounce a ball or build a tower.

Count. Record how many.
Try again slowly.
Count. Record how many. What do you notice?

2

Write.

a 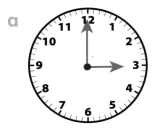   b    c    d

Read the time. Write ▢ o'clock for each clock.

3

Apply. Show the time:

a    c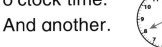

1 hour earlier   1 hour later

b 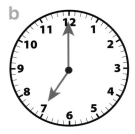   d

1 hour later   1 hour earlier

4

Think.

It is 8 o'clock in the morning.

Show an earlier o'clock time.
And another.

It is 3 o'clock in the afternoon.

Show a later o'clock time. And another.
Put the 4 times in order – earliest to latest.

Teacher's Guide

See page 63 of the *Teacher's Guide* for ideas of how to guide practice.
Work through each step together as a class to develop children's
conceptual understanding.

51 ★

You need:
- balance scales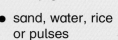
- empty containers and jugs
- sand, water, rice or pulses

My container is taller. It holds more than yours.

My container is shorter than yours but it is also wider. It might hold more than yours!

Light and heavy

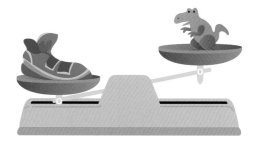   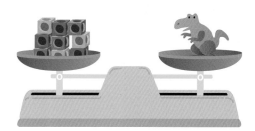

The shoe is heavier than the dinosaur.
The dinosaur is lighter than the shoe.

The scales balance.
The dinosaur weighs the same as 9 cubes.

Full and empty

These containers are full.
There is no room for any more.

These containers are empty.
There is nothing in them.

Teacher's Guide

Before working through the *Textbook*, study page 64 of the *Teacher's Guide* to see how the concepts should be introduced. Read and discuss the page with the children. Provide concrete resources to support exploration.

1 Weigh.

Choose an object.
Put it on the balance scales. Draw it.

Find 3 lighter things. Draw them.
Find 3 heavier things. Draw them.

2 Weigh and count.

Use your objects from Step 1.
Put them on the balance scales, 1 at a time.
How many cubes does each weigh?
Draw each object. Write the number of cubes.
Draw a circle around the heaviest object.
How do you know?

Object	Drawing	Number of cubes
Book	Stories	9

3 Apply.

Choose a container. Fill it. Draw it.

Find 3 containers that hold more.
Draw them.

Find 3 containers that hold less.
Draw them.

Which container holds the least?
How do you know?

4 Think.

Use your smallest and largest containers from Step 3.

Fill the smallest container. Tip the contents into the largest container. Estimate how many times you need to do this to fill the largest container. Do it. Count.

How close was your guess?

Teacher's Guide   See page 65 of the *Teacher's Guide* for ideas of how to guide practice. Work through each step together as a class to develop children's conceptual understanding.

53 ⭐

100 square games

Let's play

Start

1	2	3	4	5	6	7
11	12	13	14	15	16	17
21	22	23	24	25	26	27
31	32	33	34	35	36	37
41	42	43	44	45	46	47
51	52	53	54	55	56	57
61	62	63	64	65	66	67
71	72	73	74	75	76	77
81	82	83	84	85	86	87
91	92	93	94	95	96	97

Teacher's Guide See pages 66–7 of the *Teacher's Guide*. Explain the rules for each game and allow children to choose which to play. Encourage them to challenge themselves and practise what they have learnt in the unit.

8	9	10
18	19	20
28	29	30
38	39	40
48	49	50
58	59	60
68	69	70
78	79	80
88	89	90
98	99	100

Finish

You need:
- counters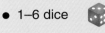
- 1–6 dice

 1 Escalators

Race to 100, moving along the escalators as you go!

 2 Too hot, too cold!

Race to 100. Watch out for the red hot and freezing blue squares!

 3 Your game

Make up your own game using the gameboard.

And finally ...

Let's review

1 Copy and complete.
These are parts of a 100 square.

You need:
- place-value cards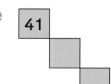

a  37

b 63

c 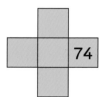 74

d 45

e 41

f 36

2

You need:
- clock with moveable hands

I woke up an hour ago.

I can't wait to get to school. Only an hour to go!

I had my breakfast an hour ago. Now I'm hungry again.

I'm hungry. 1 more hour until I have breakfast!

At what time could Jen have said each thing?

Teacher's Guide
See pages 68–9 of the *Teacher's Guide* for guidance on running each task.
Observe children to identify those who have mastered concepts and those who require further consolidation.

★**56**

3 Choose 4 similar containers.
Put them in order from smallest to largest.

smallest   largest

Fill the largest container.
Pour the contents into the next container. Be careful.

smallest   largest

The contents should overflow each time.
Were you right? If not, reorder and try again.

Did you know?

Numbers don't stop at 100. You can keep adding 1 more! We run out of names for really big numbers. We just call them all infinity.

Draw the infinity symbol. You can keep going round forever!

2 227 597 148   389 800 012   9 005 822 345

749 053 758   1 987 498   921 361 120

8 299 001   8 392 544 900   3 667 865

Adding and subtracting to 20

I love bananas! How many would be left if we had 1 each?

That's double 6! Do you know any doubles?

I wonder how many pens are still in the pack?

Teacher's Guide   Look at the pictures with the children and discuss the questions.
See pages 70–1 of the *Teacher's Guide* for key ideas to draw out.

59 ★

Doubles

You need:

- ten frames
- 1–6 dice
- interlocking cubes
- counters or other counting objects

Let's learn

Double 3 is 6. So double 4 must be 7.

Yes, double 3 is 6. But double 4 is not 7. 4 is one more than 3, but to find double 4 you cannot just add 1 more. You need to add 4 to itself. So double 4 is 4 add 4 … 8!

Doubles

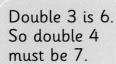 double →

double 1 = 2

$1 + 1 = 2$

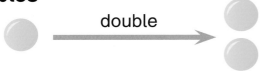 double →

double 2 = 4

$2 + 2 = 4$

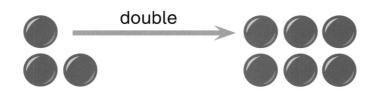 double →

double 3 = 6

$3 + 3 = 6$

A double is the same number added 2 times.

It is added **twice**.

This is 5.

This is **double** 5.

$5 + 5 = 10$

Roll a dice. Make the double.

Can you find some more doubles?

Teacher's Guide

Before working through the *Textbook*, study page 72 of the *Teacher's Guide* to see how the concepts should be introduced. Read and discuss the page with the children. Provide concrete resources to support exploration.

1 **Count.**

Double each tower. How many cubes now?

a b c  d  e  f

2 **Count.** How many?

You can use counters or cubes to help you.

a	double 4	c	double 7	e	double 5
b	double 10	d	double 3	f	double 8

3 **Measure.** Use cubes to measure the length of your hand.

What if your hand was twice as long? How many cubes long would it be?

Choose other body parts to measure with cubes. Then find double their length.

4 **Think.** Copy and complete.

Number	0	1	2	3	4	5	6	7	8	9	10
Double	0					10					

What patterns can you see?
Can you use them to work out double 11?

Teacher's Guide
See page 73 of the *Teacher's Guide* for ideas of how to guide practice. Work through each step together as a class to develop children's conceptual understanding.

61 ⭐

Adding and subtracting with 20

Let's learn

... ten, eleven, twelve, thirteen, fourteen, fifty, sixty, seventy, eighty, ninety, twenty!

You muddled up **teen** and **ty**! If there's only one 10, it's a teen number. If there's more than one 10, it's a ty number. So it is ten, eleven, twelve, thir**teen**, four**teen**, fif**teen**, six**teen**, seven**teen**, eigh**teen**, nine**teen**, twenty!

Adding 2 numbers to make 20

You can use 2 ten frames to make 20, because 10 + 10 = 20.

20 + 0 = 20 or 20 = 20 + 0

Swap 1 yellow counter for 1 red counter.

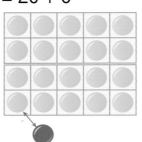

19 ⬤ + 1 ⬤ = 20 counters altogether.
19 + 1 = 20

1 ⬤ + 19 ⬤ = 20 counters altogether
1 + 19 = 20

20 counters altogether = 19 ⬤ + 1 ⬤
20 = 19 + 1

20 counters altogether = 1 ⬤ + 19 ⬤
20 = 1 + 19

Can you find all the ways to add 2 numbers to make 20?

Subtracting from 20

You can use 2 ten frames to show 20 − 0 = 20.

Slide 1 counter off a ten frame.

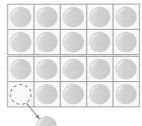

20 ⬤ − 1 ⬤ = 19 counters
20 − 1 = 19

What if 2 counters were moved off the ten frame?

Can you find all the ways to subtract a number from 20?

1 Answer these.

Put these numbers into the machine.
Find the number bonds for 20 that come out.

12  8

a   3   c   5   e   14

b   4   d   13   f   15

2 Calculate. The machine is broken and will only let you put 20 in.

First, 12 + 8 came out. Then 13 + 7.
Find all the other number bonds that will come out if you keep putting in 20.

3 Measure.

The toy and 4 cubes balance the 20 cubes. So the toy must weigh 20 − 4 cubes, 16 cubes because 20 − 4 = 16.

Find out how many cubes a toy weighs.

Use a balance scales with 20 cubes in 1 pan.

Write the number statement you used.

4 Think.

This is a large 20 fact family.

17 + 3 = 20	20 = 17 + 3
3 + 17 = 20	20 = 3 + 17
20 − 17 = 3	3 = 20 − 17
20 − 3 = 17	17 = 20 − 3

Roll 2 dice or spin a spinner to get a number less than 20. Write the large fact family for this number bond for 20.

Use 2 ten frames and some counters to help you.

Swap numbers with a friend.

Challenge each other to write the matching large 20 fact family.

Teacher's Guide

See page 75 of the *Teacher's Guide* for ideas of how to guide practice. Work through each step together as a class to develop children's conceptual understanding.

63 ★

Adding and subtracting with 11 to 19

You need:

- ten frames
- scissors
- counters
- pencil and paperclips

Let's learn

Adding is easy, you just count everything.

Yes, but it might take a long time and you could make a mistake. And what about when you can't see what you are adding? It's better to calculate. That's what number bonds are for!

Adding 2 numbers to make 15

There are 15 counters in the frames:
15 + 0 = 15 or 15 = 15 + 0

Swap 1 yellow counter for 1 red counter.

14  + 1 ⬤ = 15 counters altogether
14 + 1 = 15

1 ⬤ + 14 ◯ = 15 counters altogether
1 + 14 = 15

15 counters altogether = 14  + 1 ⬤
15 = 14 + 1

15 counters altogether = 1 ⬤ + 14 ◯
15 = 1 + 14

Can you find all the ways to add 2 numbers to make 15?

Subtracting from 15

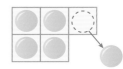

15 − 0 = 15   15 = 15 − 0

Slide 1 counter off the five frame.

15 ◯ − 1 ◯ = 14 counters.
15 − 1 = 14

What if 2 counters were moved off the five frame?

Can you find all the ways to subtract a number from 15?

Teacher's Guide

Before working through the *Textbook*, study page 76 of the *Teacher's Guide* to see how the concepts should be introduced. Read and discuss the page with the children. Provide concrete resources to support exploration.

1 Calculate.

a Write the 4 addition statements shown by this number frame for 17.

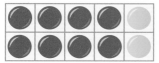 

b What if you took off the yellow counters? What if you took off the red counters? Write the 2 subtraction statements.

2

Write. Spin the spinner to choose a number. Use a pencil and a paperclip.

Use 2 ten frames to explore your number.
Write at least 10 different number statements to show what you found out.

3

Take 15 paperclips. Arrange your paperclips in 2 rows.

Use these number statements to help you record your arrangement:

☐ + ☐ = 15

15 = ☐ + ☐

15 − ☐ = ☐

☐ = 15 − ☐

Try it with 19 paperclips.

4 Think.

Sam and Jen like to skip together.

They counted their skips.
The most they did was 19 skips.
They both did at least 5 skips each time.
Sam always did 3 more skips than Jen.

How many skips could each child have done?

Use cubes or counters to help you find the answer.

For their last skip, Sam only did 2 more skips than Jen.

How many skips could each child have done?

Teacher's Guide
See page 77 of the *Teacher's Guide* for ideas of how to guide practice. Work through each step together as a class to develop children's conceptual understanding.

Twenty

Let's play

Teacher's Guide

See pages 78–9 of the *Teacher's Guide*. Explain the rules for each game and allow children to choose which to play. Encourage them to challenge themselves and practise what they have learnt in the unit.

1 **All 20**

Roll the dice to try and fill your field with 20 counters. The first player to do it wins!

2 **Empty fields**

Roll the dice to try and take away all your counters from your field. The first empty field wins!

3 **Your game**

Use the gameboard to design and play your own game.

And finally ...

1

Find all the doubles up to double 6.

Draw your own dominoes up to double 10.

How many dominoes did you need to draw?

You need:
- a set of dominoes

2

Spot the mistakes.

Write the corrected number statements.

a	14 + 3 = 20	g	13 + 8 = 20
b	20 + 20 = 20	h	20 − 18 = 12
c	11 + 10 = 20	i	5 + 5 = 20
d	20 − 6 = 4	j	20 − 8 = 11
e	12 + 7 = 20	k	20 − 1 = 17
f	20 − 12 = 9	l	20 − 20 = 20

You need:
- ten frames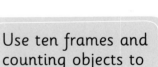
- counters or cubes

Use ten frames and counting objects to help you.

Teacher's Guide

See pages 80–1 of the *Teacher's Guide* for guidance on running each task. Observe children to identify those who have mastered concepts and those who require further consolidation.

3 Copy and complete the addition and subtraction squares.

+	augend 7	augend 9
addend 5	↓	
addend 8		

−	subtrahend 8	subtrahend
minuend 19		15
minuend 14		

+	augend	augend
addend	20	20
addend	20	20

−	subtrahend	subtrahend
minuend 20		
minuend 10		

How many different ways can you complete the last 2 squares?

Did you know?

'Twenty' is the name of a small village in Bourne, Lincolnshire, UK. Historians think the village was named after The Twenty Foot Drain, a huge drain that was built into local farmland more than 350 years ago! The drain was filled in many years ago.

Find out if there are other villages or towns with numbers in their name. Here are 3 to get you started: Sevenoaks in Kent, Seven Sisters and Seven Dials in London.

Welcome to
Twenty
Drive carefully

Money

Can you see
any 20p coins?

I wonder what
they bought and
how much it cost?

How much would 2 tomatoes cost?

How much is 1 pair of socks? What if you bought 5 pairs?

How many £10 notes are there?

Teacher's Guide
Look at the pictures with the children and discuss the questions.
See pages 82–4 of the *Teacher's Guide* for key ideas to draw out.

71★

Let's learn

I've got three coins. That's 3p altogether.

They are not all 1p coins. You've got a 2p coin and two 1p coins. Together they are worth 4p.

Our coins and notes

coins

notes

10p

Each group of coins is worth 10p.

Teacher's Guide

Before working through the *Textbook*, study page 84 of the *Teacher's Guide* to see how the concepts should be introduced. Read and discuss the page with the children. Provide concrete resources to support exploration.

1 Answer this.

Use the correct coin to buy each item.

You have 1 of each coin. Which 2 coins are left?

a b c d e f COMPOST Seeds

2 Answer this.

Find the value of each coin in pence.

Colour each on a 100 square. Which coin will not fit on the 100 square?

3 Count. How much is in each purse?

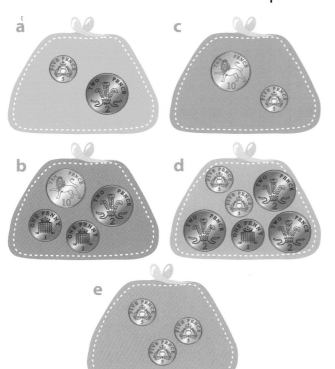

a
b
c
d
e

4 Think.

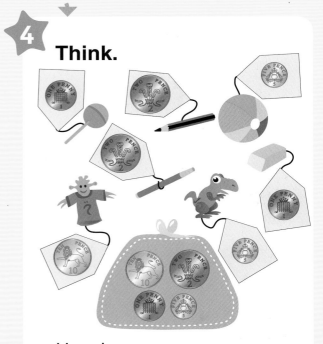

Here is your purse.

How many different ways can you buy 2 things?

What is the most you can spend? What is the least?

Teacher's Guide See page 85 of the *Teacher's Guide* for ideas of how to guide practice. Work through each step together as a class to develop children's conceptual understanding.

73 ★

Ten more, ten less

Let's learn

I can count back in tens from 100! 100, 90, 80, 17, 16, 15, 14, 13 ... Oh, that's not right!

Be careful not to mix **ty** and **teen**. Remember, teen means only 1 ten. So it's 100, 90, 80, 70, 60, 50, 40, 30, 20, 10, 0.

Counting in tens

What is 10 more than 70?

What is 10 less than 40?

1	2	3	4	5	6	7	8	9	10
11	12	13	14	15	16	17	18	19	20
21	22	23	24	25	26	27	28	29	30
31	32	33	34	35	36	37	38	39	40
41	42	43	44	45	46	47	48	49	50
51	52	53	54	55	56	57	58	59	60
61	62	63	64	65	66	67	68	69	70
71	72	73	74	75	76	77	78	79	80
81	82	83	84	85	86	87	88	89	90
91	92	93	94	95	96	97	98	99	100

10 more

10 less

Coin values

  =   =

           =

Teacher's Guide

Before working through the *Textbook*, study page 86 of the *Teacher's Guide* to see how the concepts should be introduced. Read and discuss the page with the children. Provide concrete resources to support exploration.

1 **Count.** Count in tens. Find out how many:

a apples b pens c paper cups d biscuits

  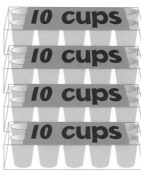 

2 **Answer these.** Read the numbers. Write the number that is 10 less.

| 20 | 100 | 70 | 10 | 80 |

Write the number that is 10 more.

| 20 | 80 | 50 | 40 | 0 |

3 **Solve.**

How many 10p coins are worth the same as each coin or note?

4 **Think.**

Sam has made £1 with 4 coins.
Find 3 different ways to make £1.

Use as many
10p, 20p or 50p
coins as you like.

Teacher's Guide
See page 87 of the *Teacher's Guide* for ideas of how to guide practice.
Work through each step together as a class to develop children's
conceptual understanding.

75 ★

You need:
- ten frames
- 100 square
- cubes
- money (coins)

I can count in twos! 2, 4, 6, 8, 10, 11, 12, 13, 14, 15!

You did well to 10, then counted in ones. It should be 2, 4, 6, 8, 10, 12, 14, 16, 18, 20.

Counting in twos – even numbers

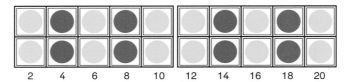

2   4   6   8   10   12   14   16   18   20

When we count in twos from zero, the numbers are called even numbers.

2p → 4p → 6p → 8p → 10p → 12p   12p altogether

Even and odd numbers

1	2	3	4	5	6	7	8	9	10
11	12	13	14	15	16	17	18	19	20
21	22	23	24	25	26	27	28	29	30
31	32	33	34	35	36	37	38	39	40
41	42	43	44	45	46	47	48	49	50
51	52	53	54	55	56	57	58	59	60
61	62	63	64	65	66	67	68	69	70
71	72	73	74	75	76	77	78	79	80
81	82	83	84	85	86	87	88	89	90
91	92	93	94	95	96	97	98	99	100

1	2	3	4	5	6	7	8	9	10
11	12	13	14	15	16	17	18	19	20
21	22	23	24	25	26	27	28	29	30
31	32	33	34	35	36	37	38	39	40
41	42	43	44	45	46	47	48	49	50
51	52	53	54	55	56	57	58	59	60
61	62	63	64	65	66	67	68	69	70
71	72	73	74	75	76	77	78	79	80
81	82	83	84	85	86	87	88	89	90
91	92	93	94	95	96	97	98	99	100

Count in twos. Colour each number on a 100 square.

Odd numbers have 1 left over when put into twos. Try it using cubes.

Teacher's Guide

Before working through the *Textbook*, study page 88 of the *Teacher's Guide* to see how the concepts should be introduced. Read and discuss the page with the children. Provide concrete resources to support exploration.

★76

1 **Copy and complete.** Draw each money path by counting on or back in steps of 2p.

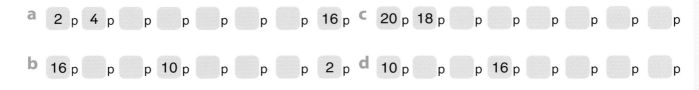

a [2]p [4]p [ ]p [ ]p [ ]p [ ]p [ ]p [16]p   c [20]p [18]p [ ]p [ ]p [ ]p [ ]p [ ]p [ ]p

b [16]p [ ]p [ ]p [10]p [ ]p [ ]p [ ]p [2]p   d [10]p [ ]p [ ]p [16]p [ ]p [ ]p [ ]p [ ]p

2 **Copy and complete.** Draw the houses. Write the house numbers.

Odd Street — ① ③ ○ ○ ○ ○ ○ ○ ○ ○

Even Street — ㉚ ㉜ ○ ○ ○ ○ ○ ○ ○ ○

3 **Apply.** Sort the price labels.

Make 2 groups – odd or even.
Write 2p more than the odd amounts.
Write 2p less than the even amounts.

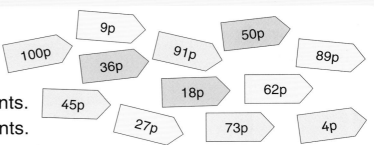

9p 50p 100p 91p 89p 36p 45p 18p 62p 27p 73p 4p

4 **Think.**

Which are true? How do you know?

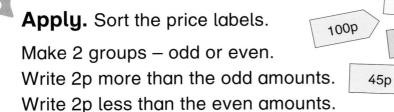

We have more odd value coins than *even* value coins.

2 more than an odd number is always an odd number.

2 less than an even number is always an odd number.

Teacher's Guide

See page 89 of the *Teacher's Guide* for ideas of how to guide practice. Work through each step together as a class to develop children's conceptual understanding.

Coin race

Let's play

Start

1

2

3

move back 2 spaces 4

5

move on 2 spaces 6

20

19

18

17

move on 2 spaces 16

move back 10 spaces 15

14

21

22

23

24

25

move on 2 spaces 26

27

28

42

41

40

39

38

37

move on 2 spaces 36

43

44

45

move on 2 spaces 46

47

48

49

50

Teacher's Guide See pages 90–1 of the *Teacher's Guide*. Explain the rules for each game and allow children to choose which to play. Encourage them to challenge themselves and practise what they have learnt in the unit.

7

8

9

move on
10 spaces
10

13

12

11

29

move on
10 spaces
30

31

32

move back
10 spaces
35

34

33

You need:

- 2p and
  10p coins
- 1–6 dice
- counters

1 **How much?**

Race to the end and find
out who has collected the
most money! Follow the
instructions along the way.

2 **2p or 10p?**

Race to collect 2p or 10p
coins – the player with the
most coins at the end is the
winner!

3 **Your game**

Design your own game.
Explain the rules and play
with a partner.

And finally ...

Let's review

1

Make these amounts.

a   2p

b   5p

c   10p

d   20p

e   50p

f   £1

g   £2

h   £5

i   £10

J   £20

Use more than 1 coin or note each time.

2

These fishermen have even numbers on their tops.
On the *Seventy* ship, the fishermen's tops must have 7 tens.
Which numbers could they have?

Today the fishermen have caught lots of fish!
It is an odd number with 7 tens. How many fish could that be?

A new ship is called *Sixty*.
Which even numbers could the fishermen have on their tops?

They have caught an odd number of fish with 6 tens.
How many fish could that be?

Teacher's Guide

See pages 92–3 of the *Teacher's Guide* for guidance on running each task.
Observe children to identify those who have mastered concepts and those who require further consolidation.

3 Which of these sentences are true? How do you know?

Even numbers always have 1, 3, 5, 7, or 9 in the ones place.

Odd numbers always have 0, 2, 4, 6, or 8 in the ones place.

Even numbers always have 0, 2, 4, 6, or 8 in the ones place.

Odd numbers always have 1, 3, 5, 7, or 9 in the ones place.

Did you know?

One of the rarest British coins is the penny made in 1933. Only 6 or 7 were ever made.

If you had one it would be worth a lot of money now!

Groups and rows

What do you notice?

How many people can sit here?

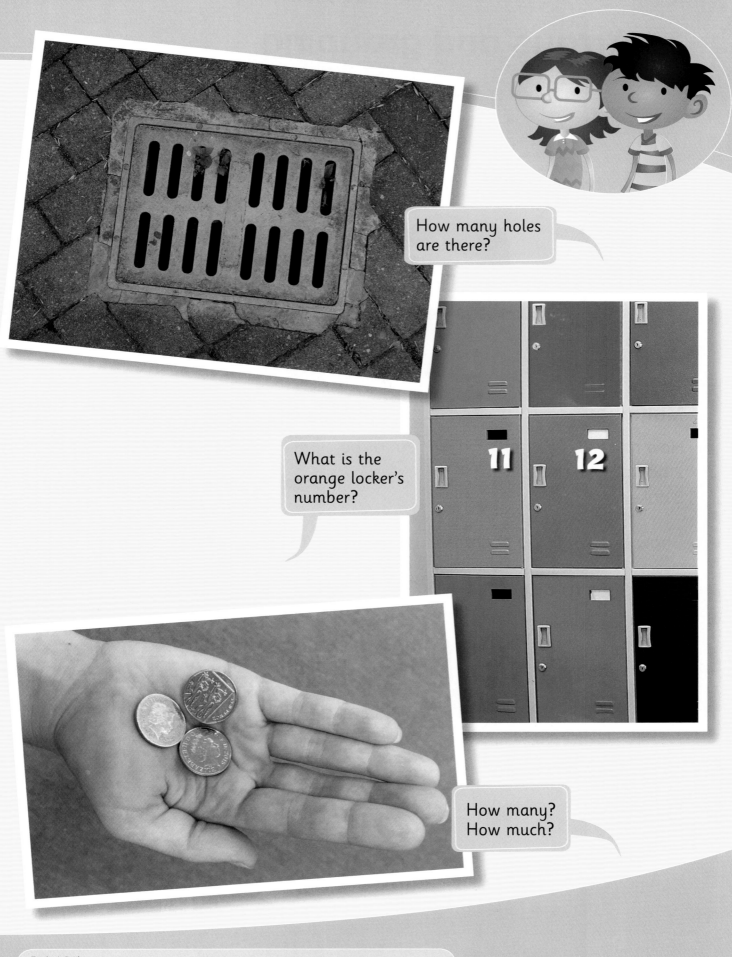

How many holes are there?

What is the orange locker's number?

How many? How much?

Teacher's Guide Look at the pictures with the children and discuss the questions.
See pages 94–5 of the *Teacher's Guide* for key ideas to draw out.

83

Let's learn

I arranged my 6 sweets into 2 rows. 1 row has 4 sweets, the other row has 2. This is an array.

No. An array must have the same number in each row.

You need:
- cubes
- toy figures or animals
- counters
- plastic cups

Multiplying

How many altogether?

2 boys.

3 cakes each.

An array

Show 2 more cakes each. How many altogether now?

Grouping to divide

There are 20 children. How many groups of 2?

There are 20 cubes in groups of 2. How many groups are there?

Can you make groups of 5 and 10? How many groups for each?

Teacher's Guide

Before working through the *Textbook*, study page 96 of the *Teacher's Guide* to see how the concepts should be introduced. Read and discuss the page with the children. Provide concrete resources to support exploration.

1 **Count.** Put a counter in each space.

How many in each row?
How many altogether?

a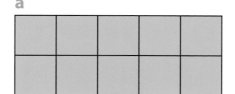

b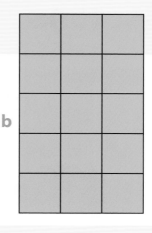

c

2 **Count.**

Put into groups of 2. How many groups of 2?

3 **Apply.**

Use paper and cups.
Each tray holds 2 cups.
How many cups?

a Tray   Tray   Tray

b Tray   Tray   Tray   Tray

c Tray   Tray   Tray   Tray   Tray

Try different numbers of cups on the tray. Draw it.

4 **Think.**

Pencils are sold in boxes of 10. Buy everyone in your class a pencil. How many boxes?

Put the pencils into arrays.

Teacher's Guide

See page 97 of the *Teacher's Guide* for ideas of how to guide practice. Work through each step together as a class to develop children's conceptual understanding.

85 ⭐

Twos, tens and sharing

You need:
- ten frames
- counters or cubes
- playing cards
- 1p coins   1p
- modelling dough

Let's learn

I have 4 stickers. We can share them. You have 1. I have 3.

In maths, share equally. Everyone gets the same amount. 1 for you, 1 for me. 1 for you, 1 for me. That's 2 each.

Counting objects in twos or tens

Count in twos. Group objects into twos to count quickly.

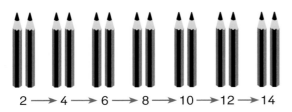

2 → 4 → 6 → 8 → 10 → 12 → 14

2, 4, 6, 8, 10, 12, 14. There are 14 pencils.

How many pencils in 8 groups of 2?

Group into tens.

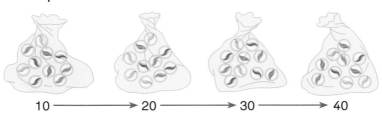

10 → 20 → 30 → 40

10, 20, 30, 40. There are 40 marbles.

How many marbles in 5 bags of 10?

Sharing

There are 12 cards. 3 children are playing.

How many cards will each child get?

Teacher's Guide

Before working through the *Textbook*, study page 98 of the *Teacher's Guide* to see how the concepts should be introduced. Read and discuss the page with the children. Provide concrete resources to support exploration.

1 Count.

How many cubes in each row?

How many cubes in each tray?

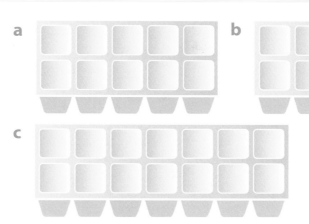

2 Answer this. Share the coins. How many coins go in each money box?

3 Apply. Count in tens. How many cubes long is each snake? Make a snake 70 cubes long.

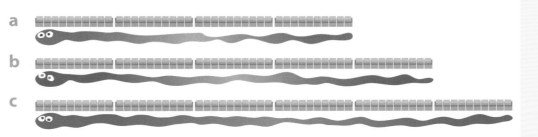

4 Think.

How can you share the £2 coins between the money boxes?

How much money will be in each box?

Teacher's Guide

See page 99 of the *Teacher's Guide* for ideas of how to guide practice. Work through each step together as a class to develop children's conceptual understanding.

87 ★

Arrays!

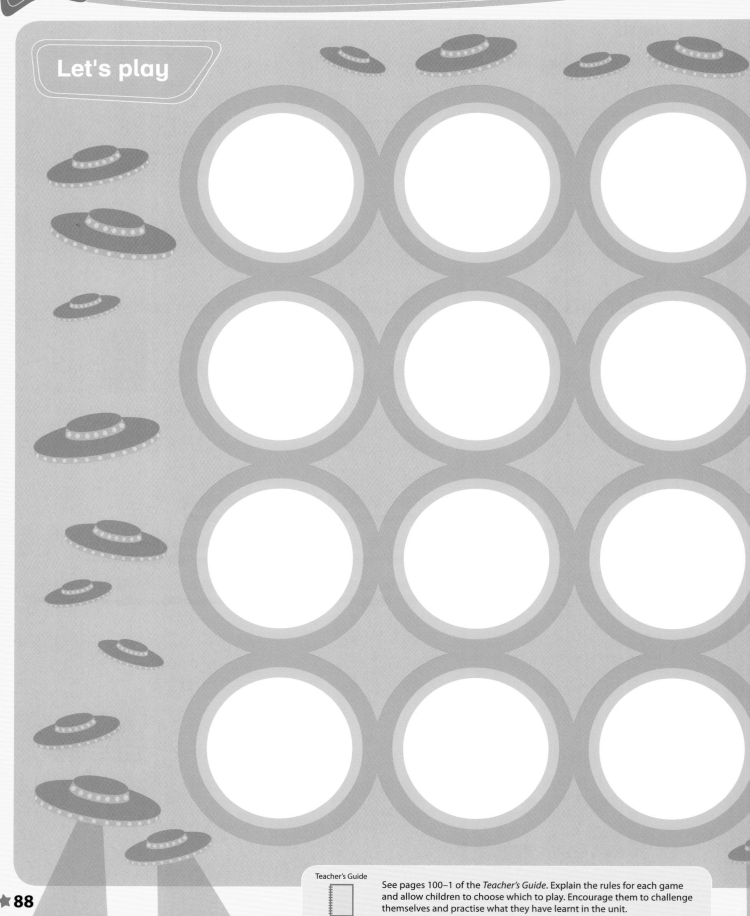

Let's play

Teacher's Guide

See pages 100–1 of the *Teacher's Guide*. Explain the rules for each game and allow children to choose which to play. Encourage them to challenge themselves and practise what they have learnt in the unit.

1 **Grouping race**

Race to make groups of counters in your column. The first one to finish and say how many counters is the winner!

2 **Array maker**

Take turns to build arrays. The winner is the last player able to place a counter!

3 **Your game**

Make up your own game using the gameboard.

89 ⭐

And finally ...

Let's review

1

Class 1 has been collecting 1p coins for charity.
How much money have the children collected?

You need:
- 1p coins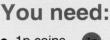

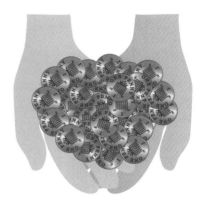

How many 1p coins you can hold?
Arrange the 1p coins in rows of 2.

Can you count them
without counting each coin?

2

20 children want to play sports.

Each team must have the same number of children.
How many children should be in each team?

You need:
- 20 small toys

Teacher's Guide
See pages 102–3 of the *Teacher's Guide* for guidance on running each task.
Observe children to identify those who have mastered concepts and those who
require further consolidation.

3 The flowers are being put into 2 vases.
Each vase must have the same number of flowers.

How many flowers in each vase?

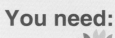

You need:
- flowers
- vases
- camera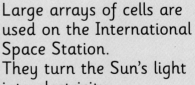

What if there were more flowers?
Make up your own problem:
- How many flowers will you use?
- How many vases?
- How many flowers in each vase?

Did you know?

You will find arrays everywhere – even in space!

Large arrays of cells are used on the International Space Station.
They turn the Sun's light into electricity.

Measuring

Would I be able to stand up in the water?

Whose clothes could these be?

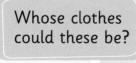

Teacher's Guide
Look at the pictures with the children and discuss the questions.
See pages 104–5 of the *Teacher's Guide* for key ideas to draw out.

93 ★

Measuring length and height

Let's learn

Look! The pencils are both the same length.

No they are not. Match up the other ends. See? The red one is shorter.

You need:
- ten rods
- 30 cm rulers
- metre sticks
- modelling dough

Measuring using centimetres and metres

We measure everyday lengths and heights with a ruler, metre stick, tape measure or trundle wheel.

Length and height is measured in centimetres and metres.

You write **cm** for centimetres and **m** for metres.

100 centimetres = 1 metre

1 metre is as long as 10 of these rulers.

Measuring with a ruler

A ruler is just like a number line.
The space between each mark is exactly 1 cm long.

This pencil is 7 cm long.

Ruler rules

Line up the end of the object with 0 on the ruler.

Be careful! Sometimes 0 is not written on the ruler so use the beginning of the ruler instead.

How far along the ruler is the other end of the object?
Read the scale carefully, to the nearest centimetre.

Teacher's Guide

Before working through the *Textbook,* study page 106 of the *Teacher's Guide* to see how the concepts should be introduced. Read and discuss the page with the children. Provide concrete resources to support exploration.

1 Find and measure.

Use a 30 cm ruler to measure the length or height of 6 objects in your classroom.

Which is the longest?

Which is the shortest? How do you know?

Object	Length or height (cm)

2 How many?

Look at Tyler in question 3. He is 10 cm long. Use Tyler to measure some lengths and heights.

Write these in Tylers and centimetres.

How many 10 cm Tylers are the same length as a 30 cm ruler?

How many 10 cm Tylers are the same length as a metre stick?

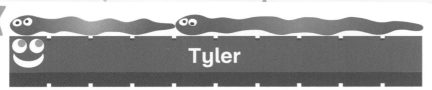

Tyler

3 Make and measure.

Make a 10 cm Tyler from a ten rod.

Make pairs of dough worms that are 10 cm long when put end to end.

Use your 10 cm Tyler to check.

Record the lengths of the worms like this:

▢ cm + ▢ cm = 10 cm

What do you notice?

4 Think.

Use a metre stick to find 3 things that are a bit shorter than 1 m.

Draw or write the name of the objects.

Record how tall or long they are.

Teacher's Guide
See page 107 of the *Teacher's Guide* for ideas of how to guide practice. Work through each step together as a class to develop children's conceptual understanding.

95 ⭐

You need:
- balance scales
- kitchen scales
- weights
- fruit

Let's learn

Big things are heavy.

Big doesn't mean heavy. A huge balloon doesn't weigh much but a small rock can be heavy.

Measuring using grams and kilograms

You measure mass in grams and kilograms. You write **g** for grams and **kg** for kilograms. 1000 grams = 1 kilogram

Almost everything is heavier than 1 gram!

All of these things have a mass of about 1 g.

All of these things have a mass of 1 kg.

The toy is lighter than 1 kg so the 1 kg mass presses down harder on the scales.

The bag of rice weighs 1 kg. This is the same as the 1 kg mass so the scales balance.

The melon is heavier than the 1 kg so it presses down harder on the scales.

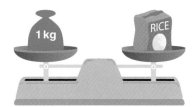

Teacher's Guide

Before working through the *Textbook*, study page 108 of the *Teacher's Guide* to see how the concepts should be introduced. Read and discuss the page with the children. Provide concrete resources to support exploration.

1

Measure and draw.

Find and draw 3 things with a mass of:

a   less than 1 kg.

b   more than 1 kg.

c   about the same as 1 kg.

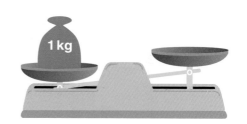

2

Measure and record.

Measure the mass of some everyday classroom objects.

What is the mass of each object?
Which object is the heaviest?
Which object is the lightest?
How do you know?

Object	Mass (g or kg)

3

Measure.

A shop sells 1 kg bowls of fruits.

A bowl can have 1, 2 or lots of different kinds of fruit in it.

Make 3 different 1 kg bowls of fruit for the shop.

Draw, write a list or take a photo of each bowl.

4

Think.

Order the objects from lightest to heaviest.

The cat has eaten the fish!
What is the mass of the cat now?

The dog has eaten the chicken!
What is the mass of the dog now?

You carried 10 kg. Which objects could you have carried? Find 2 different solutions.

Teacher's Guide

See page 109 of the *Teacher's Guide* for ideas of how to guide practice. Work through each step together as a class to develop children's conceptual understanding.

97 ★

Measuring capacity and volume

Let's learn

It says 100 millilitres on the label. There must be a liquid inside.

The 100 millilitres just tells you how much is in the container. My dad's shaving foam has millilitres on the label. So does my sun cream and toothpaste.

Volume

Volume is the amount of space an object fills.

Which boxes could the kangaroo fit in?
What about the mouse?

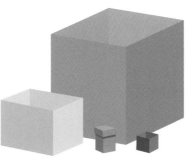

Measuring capacity

Capacity is the amount a container can hold. You measure capacity in millilitres and litres. You write **ml** for millilitres and **l** for litres.

All of these things contain 1 l.
They have a capacity of 1 l.

1000 millilitres = 1 litre
1 drop from a pipette = 1 ml

That means the 1-litre containers can hold 1000 drops from the pipette!

Teacher's Guide

Before working through the *Textbook*, study page 110 of the *Teacher's Guide* to see how the concepts should be introduced. Read and discuss the page with the children. Provide concrete resources to support exploration.

1 Answer this.

Which ball will fit in each box?

Now choose 3 classroom objects and find a box just the right size for each one.

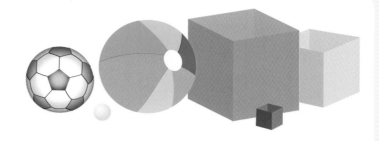

2 Find and draw.

Find containers with a capacity of more than 1 litre. Check by pouring in 1 l of water.

Draw the containers that hold more than a litre.

Show where 1 l of water comes to in the container.

3 Measure.

Estimate how many litres each container will hold.

Order from smallest to greatest capacity.

Use a 1-litre jug to check your estimates.

Do you need to change the order?

4 Think.

Estimate how many times you can fill a small container using 1 l of water. Measure this.

Choose 2 more containers to do the same with.

How will you record your estimates and measurements?

How close were they?

Teacher's Guide

See page 111 of the *Teacher's Guide* for ideas of how to guide practice. Work through each step together as a class to develop children's conceptual understanding.

99 ⭐

Vegetable soup

Let's play

START

1 kg potatoes

1 l water

1 kg sweetcorn

1 kg parsnips

1 l water

1 kg watercress

1 kg onions

1 kg peas

1 l water

1 kg sweet potato

Teacher's Guide

See pages 112–13 of the *Teacher's Guide*. Explain the rules for each game and allow children to choose which to play. Encourage them to challenge themselves and practise what they have learnt in the unit.

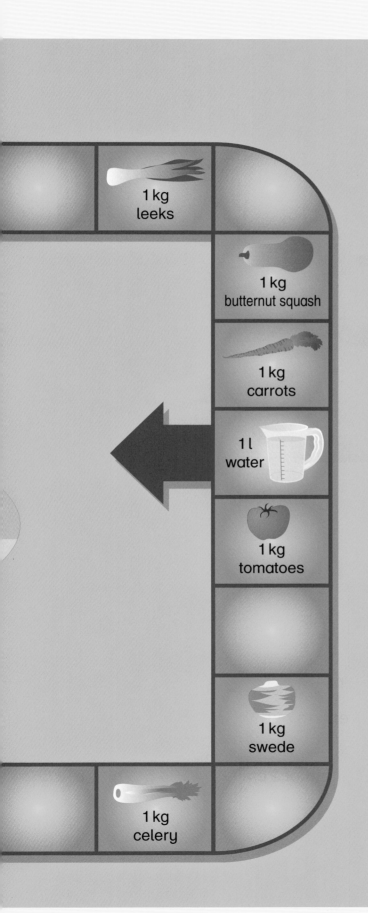

1 kg
leeks

1 kg
butternut squash

1 kg
carrots

1 l
water

1 kg
tomatoes

1 kg
swede

1 kg
celery

1 Vegetable harvest

Race to collect vegetables and water to make soup. The first one to the kitchen is the winner.

2 Designer soup

Race to collect the ingredients for your own soup. The first one to the kitchen is the winner.

3 Your game

Design your own game. Explain the rules and play with a partner.

And finally ...

Let's review

1

Measure and record the length of each pencil.

You need:
- 30 cm ruler

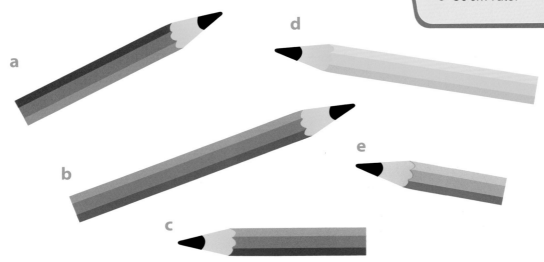

a

d

b

e

c

Then find the combined lengths.

f   Red pencil + green pencil =

g   Red pencil + blue pencil =

h   Red pencil + blue pencil + yellow pencil =

i   Red pencil + yellow pencil + brown pencil =

j   Which 2 pencils are 11 cm long if laid end to end?
     Find more than 1 solution.

k   Which 2 pencils have a difference in length of 2 cm?
     Find more than 1 solution.

Teacher's Guide

See pages 114–15 of the *Teacher's Guide* for guidance on running each task.
Observe children to identify those who have mastered concepts and those who
require further consolidation.

2

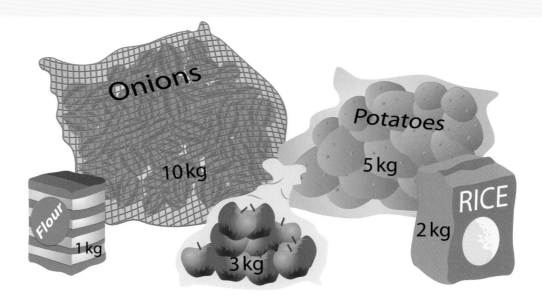

Onions 10 kg

Potatoes 5 kg

RICE 2 kg

3 kg

Flour 1 kg

Order these from lightest to heaviest.

3

Draw or name some things that would be measured in centimetres or metres, grams or kilograms, millilitres or litres at school.
Now do the same for your home and the supermarket.

Did you know?

A newborn baby usually has a mass of between 3 and 4 kilograms.

Newborn elephants are about 90 kg and a kangaroo, or joey, can have a mass as small as 1 g. But a hippo, also called a calf, has a mass of at least 25 kg and is born underwater!

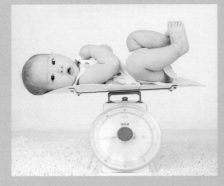
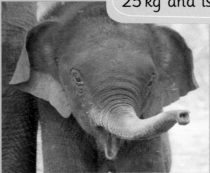

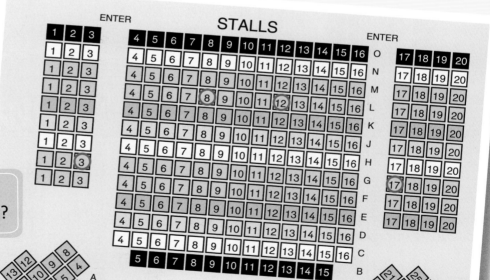

MAY						
SUN	MON	TUE	WED	THU	FRI	SAT
28	29	30	1	2	3	4
5	6	7	8	9	10	11
12	13	14	15	16	17	18
19	20	21	22	23	24	25
26	27	28	29	30	31	1
2	3	4	5	6	7	8

We're going to visit Granny on 18th. How many days is that? How many weeks?

Are those squares seats?

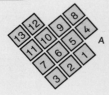

How can we tell the time on this clock?

Which hand is missing?

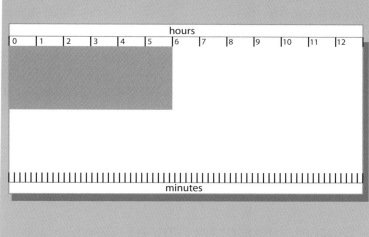

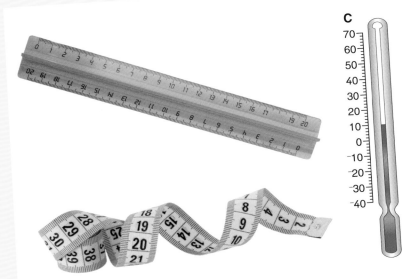

Do you think these are all number lines?

Teacher's Guide

Look at the pictures with the children and discuss the questions.
See pages 116–17 of the *Teacher's Guide* for key ideas to draw out.

105 ★

Adding and subtracting on a number line

Let's learn

When I added 7 and 5 on a number line, I ended up on 11.

That's not right, you only did 4 jumps! You counted 7 as a jump but you were already on 7. To add 5 you need 5 jumps. 7 add 5 is 12.

Adding on a number line

Jump forward the right number of steps on a number line to add.

$7 + 5 = $

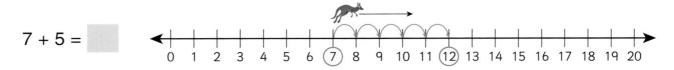

Start at 7, count on 5 more. $7 + 5 = 12$

Remember, augend + addend = sum

Subtracting on a number line

Jump back the right number of steps on a number line to subtract.

$12 - 5 = $

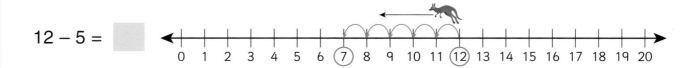

Start at 12, count back 5 less. $12 - 5 = 7$

Remember, minuend − subtrahend = difference

What do you notice about the jumps on both number lines?

Teacher's Guide

Before working through the *Textbook*, study page 118 of the *Teacher's Guide* to see how the concepts should be introduced. Read and discuss the page with the children. Provide concrete resources to support exploration.

1

Answer these. Roll a dice to find the augend or addend for each number statement. Use a number line to find the sum.

a   13 + ☐ = ☐

c   9 + ☐ = ☐

e   14 + ☐ = ☐

b   ☐ + 7 = ☐

d   ☐ + 9 = ☐

f   ☐ + 8 = ☐

2

Answer these. Roll a dice to find the subtrahend for each number statement. Use a number line to find the difference.

a   13 – ☐ = ☐

c   18 – ☐ = ☐

e   17 – ☐ = ☐

b   9 – ☐ = ☐

d   15 – ☐ = ☐

f   8 – ☐ = ☐

3

Apply.

Shuffle a set of digit cards. Turn over the top two cards. Decide whether to add or subtract or you could do both.

Use a ruler as a number line then write the sum or difference. You are adding or subtracting centimetres, so remember to show this in your recording.

4

Think.

Show these calculations on a number line. Can you write 2 number statements for each speech bubble?

I started at 9 and needed 7 jumps.

I started at 12 and needed 8 jumps.

I started at 15 and needed 4 jumps.

Teacher's Guide   See page 119 of the *Teacher's Guide* for ideas of how to guide practice. Work through each step together as a class to develop children's conceptual understanding.

107 ★

When and where?

Let's learn

It's 9 12 o'clock.

You're right, it is 9 o'clock. You don't need to say the 12. 'O'clock' means the minute hand is pointing to the 12.

How many days?

MONDAY	TUESDAY	WEDNESDAY	THURSDAY	FRIDAY	SATURDAY	SUNDAY
1	2	3	4	5	6	7
⑧	9	10	11	12	13	14
15	16	17	18	⑲	20	21
22	23	24	25	26	27	28
29	30					

Today is Monday 8th. We go to the Wildlife Park on Friday 19th. How many days is that?

$19 - 8 = 11$

$8 + 11 = 19$

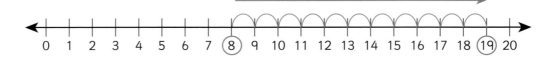

At the Wildlife Park

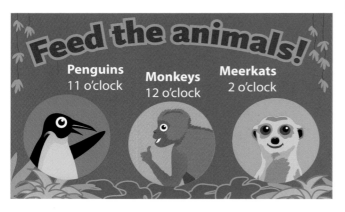

Feed the animals!

Penguins 11 o'clock

Monkeys 12 o'clock

Meerkats 2 o'clock

- Arrive 10 o'clock
- Bus leaves 3 o'clock
- Book school room for lunch 12 o'clock or 1 o'clock?

Class trip timetable

10 o'clock	Arrive at Wildlife Park
11 o'clock	Feed the penguins
12 o'clock	Feed the monkeys
2 o'clock	Feed the meerkats
3 o'clock	Catch bus back

Why must the teacher book the school room for 1 o'clock?

Teacher's Guide

Before working through the *Textbook*, study page 120 of the *Teacher's Guide* to see how the concepts should be introduced. Read and discuss the page with the children. Provide concrete resources to support exploration.

1. Draw.

Draw the clock for each time.
Use a model clock to help you.

Date: **Monday 17th April**

9 o'clock   Take 🐕 to the vet
11 o'clock   Shopping delivered
12 o'clock   Lunch with Sammy
4 o'clock   Meet George and Sophie
             in the park
6 o'clock   Ring Granddad
7 o'clock   A new TV show starts

2. Draw.

Draw and write the time
2 hours earlier and 2 hours
later than each time.

8 o'clock

5 o'clock

3. Apply.

MONDAY	TUESDAY	WEDNESDAY	THURSDAY	FRIDAY	SATURDAY	SUNDAY
			1	2	3	4
5	6	7	8	9	10	11
12	13	14	15	16	17	18
19	20	21	22	23	24	25
26	27	28	29	30	31	

Today is 5th. We go on holiday on 17th. How many days is that?

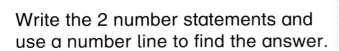

Write the 2 number statements and use a number line to find the answer.

4. Think.

Draw clocks and write the times for each of the clues.
Use a number line to help you.

Start

🕙	**1** 2 hours later 10 o'clock	**2** 1 hour earlier
		3 2 hours earlier
6 1 hour later	**5** 2 hours earlier	**4** 1 hour earlier
7 2 hours earlier		
8 1 hour later		

Finish

Teacher's Guide
See page 121 of the *Teacher's Guide* for ideas of how to guide practice. Work through each step together as a class to develop children's conceptual understanding.

109 ★

Time o'clock

0 1 2 3 4 5 6 7 8 9 10 11 12

Teacher's Guide

See pages 122–3 of the *Teacher's Guide*. Explain the rules for each game and allow children to choose which to play. Encourage them to challenge themselves and practise what they have learnt in the unit.

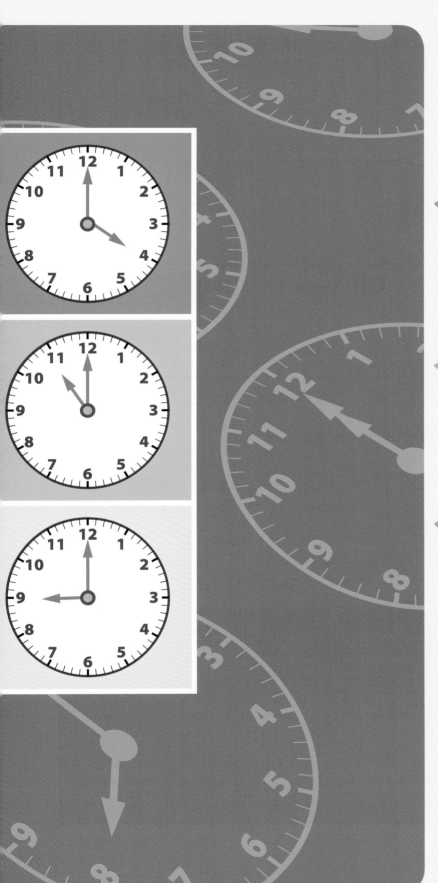

- 12 counters each
- two 1–6 dice
- coin 2p

1 **Every hour**

Take turns to roll the dice and add or subtract the numbers. Can you place a counter on every o'clock?

2 **1 o'clock or 12 o'clock?**

Toss the coin to help you reach 1 o'clock or 12 o'clock from a 6 o'clock start. Where will you end up?

3 **Your game**

Make up your own game using the gameboard.

And finally ...

Let's review

1

Complete the number statements for each number line.

11 ◆ 5 = 6   6 ◆ 5 = 11

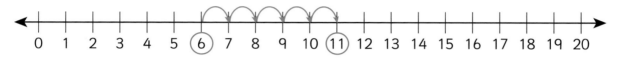

4 + ▢ = 15   15 − ▢ = 4

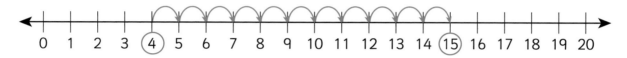

What number statements are shown on this number line?

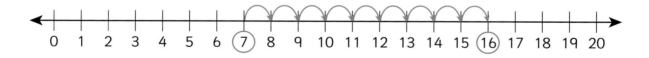

2

The vet booked in all these cats for tomorrow morning.

Put the appointment times in order.

Which cats are arriving at each appointment time?

Tiddles 11 o'clock	Paws 8 o'clock	Tigger 9 o'clock	Gizmo 10 o'clock	Muffin 8 o'clock
Bandit 9 o'clock	Pumpkin 12 o'clock	Princess 11 o'clock	Muffin 12 o'clock	Chester 10 o'clock
Shadow 12 o'clock	Socks 10 o'clock	Simba 8 o'clock	Patch 9 o'clock	Peanut 11 o'clock

Teacher's Guide

See pages 124–5 of the *Teacher's Guide* for guidance on running each task. Observe children to identify those who have mastered concepts and those who require further consolidation.

$17 - 5 = 12$ $20 - 3 = 17$

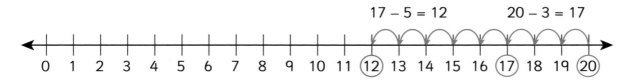

Start at 20. Roll a dice to tell you how many to subtract on the number line.

Draw in the jumps and write the number statement.

Keep rolling the dice and subtracting the number. How many subtraction calculations can you make?

Try again on 2 more number lines. Did you land on 0?

Use another 3 number lines and a dice to explore addition in the same way.

Did you land on 20?

Did you know?

Until around 200 years ago, clocks only had 1 hand, the hour hand. This 1-handed clock is on Westminster Abbey in London.

Is it easier to tell the time on a 1-handed clock?

Unit 10

Building towers and moving shapes

What shape containers can you see?

What shapes can you see?

Where is the sugar?

I wonder how they know where each box is?

Can you see the repeating pattern?

Teacher's Guide
Look at the pictures with the children and discuss the questions.
See pages 126–7 of the *Teacher's Guide* for key ideas to draw out.

115 ★

Let's learn

This red shape is a cylinder. I'm not sure about the blue shape – it's very thin.

The blue shape has 2 faces that are circles and 1 curved surface. It is a cylinder as well!

What makes a 3-D shape?

A cylinder has 2 faces that are circles.
They are joined by a curved surface.
Think about what makes a cuboid. What about a cube? A sphere?

Look at the 2 pyramids.
What is the same about them?
What is different?

Building stable towers

Which tower will be harder to knock over?

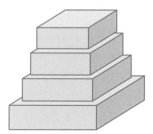

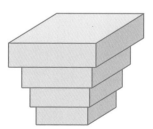

Strong towers have a wide base. They are **stable**.

Top-heavy towers are **unstable**.
The shapes get wider as you go up.

Teacher's Guide

Before working through the *Textbook*, study page 128 of the *Teacher's Guide* to see how the concepts should be introduced. Read and discuss the page with the children. Provide concrete resources to support exploration.

1 Describe.

Look at the pairs of shapes.

Say 1 thing that is the same.

Say 1 thing that is different.

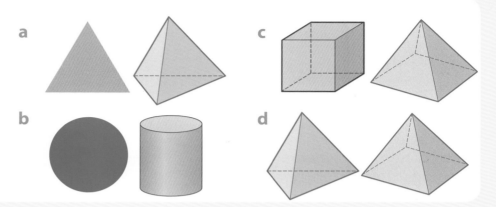

a b c d

2 Explain.

These towers would fall down! Explain why.

Can you change the towers to make them stable?

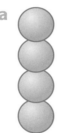

a b c

3 Build.

Choose 5 food containers. Make sure you have at least:

- 1 cube
- 1 cuboid
- 1 cylinder.

Build the tallest tower you can. Measure its height.

Build the shortest tower you can. Use all 5 shapes. Measure again.

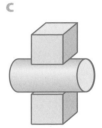

4 Think.

Use 3-D shapes to build a tower. 1 side must have only square faces.

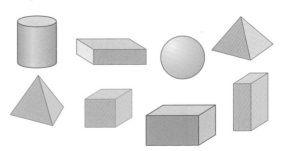

What shapes have you used? Make a list.

Teacher's Guide

See page 129 of the *Teacher's Guide* for ideas of how to guide practice. Work through each step together as a class to develop children's conceptual understanding.

117 ⭐

You need:
- 3-D shapes
- 2-D shapes

Let's learn

You said 'Forward 4 steps, turn left, forward 3 steps'. I said 'Turn left, forward 3 steps, turn right, forward 4 steps'. But we ended up at the same place. That can't be right!

It is right. You went one way and I went the other.

Giving directions

Look at how the dog can reach the kennel.

Green: forward 3, turn right, forward 3

Pink: forward 1, turn right, forward 3, turn left, forward 2

Purple: forward 1, turn right, forward 1, turn left, forward 2, turn right, forward 2

The routes are all correct.

The green one has the fewest instructions.

Finish

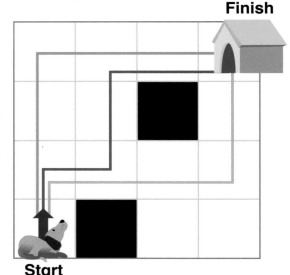

Start

Describing repeating patterns

Look at this pattern.

It repeats every 5 objects.

The first and second shapes are the same.

The fourth and fifth shapes are the same.

What will the next shape be?

What is the mistake in this pattern?

Teacher's Guide

Before working through the *Textbook*, study page 130 of the *Teacher's Guide* to see how the concepts should be introduced. Read and discuss the page with the children. Provide concrete resources to support exploration.

Let's practise

 1

Describe.

How could you move each shape from its Start to Finish?

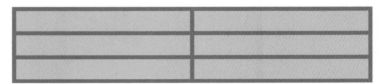

 2

Draw.

Copy the shelves and draw the food on them like this:

- box of breakfast cereal on the bottom shelf at the right
- box of tea bags on the left-hand side of the middle shelf
- box of biscuits above the breakfast cereal
- tin of sweetcorn above the biscuits
- tin of baked beans below the tea bags
- your choice of shopping to the left of the sweetcorn.

3

Apply. Use a label for each shape and find a place to hide it.

Write a sentence for each one.

Give a friend your sentences to find the shapes.

Use these words:

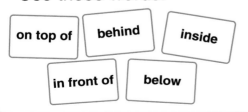

The cuboid is on top of the maths cupboard.

4

Think.

Make a repeating pattern of 5 2-D shapes.

Keep it hidden.

Describe your pattern so your partner can make it.

Try it without saying the shape names.

Teacher's Guide

See page 131 of the *Teacher's Guide* for ideas of how to guide practice. Work through each step together as a class to develop children's conceptual understanding.

Building towers!

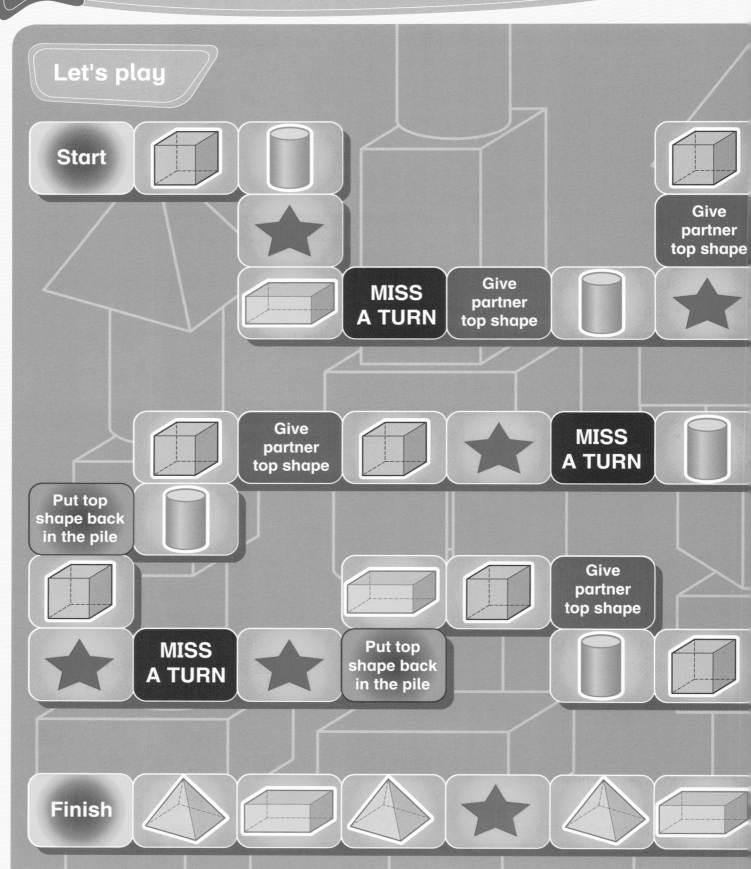

Let's play

Start

MISS A TURN

Give partner top shape

Give partner top shape

Give partner top shape

Put top shape back in the pile

MISS A TURN

Give partner top shape

MISS A TURN

Put top shape back in the pile

Finish

Teacher's Guide
See pages 132–3 of the *Teacher's Guide*. Explain the rules for each game and allow children to choose which to play. Encourage them to challenge themselves and practise what they have learnt in the unit.

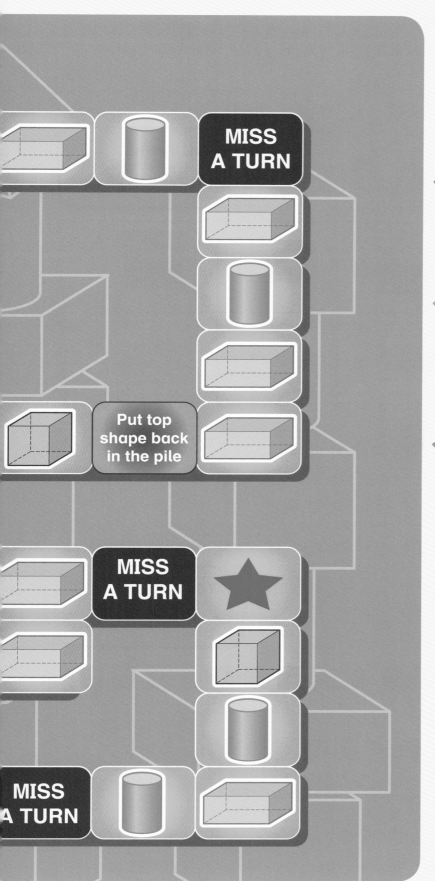

MISS A TURN

Put top shape back in the pile

MISS A TURN

MISS A TURN

1 Tall towers

Collect 3-D shapes to build tall towers.

2 Star towers

Build a tower with 3-D shapes. Tossing a coin may help you – or not!

3 Your game

Make up your own game using the gameboard.

And finally ...

Let's review

1

You need:
- 1–10 dice

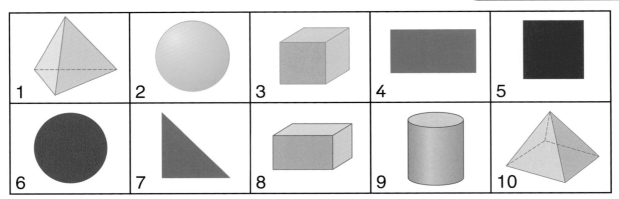

Roll the dice twice to find 2 shapes.

Find 1 property that is the same for the 2 shapes.

Find 1 property that is different.

2

Look at these repeating patterns.
Find and describe the mistake.

You need:
- 2-D shapes

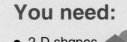

Make your own repeating pattern – with a mistake.
See if your friend can spot it.

Teacher's Guide

See pages 134–5 of the *Teacher's Guide* for guidance on running each task.
Observe children to identify those who have mastered concepts and those who
require further consolidation.

Music systems		DAB Radios		Headphones
	Mobile phones		Cordless phones	
ROBOT Start & Finish			TVs	
Computers		Computer tablets		Games consoles

a This is a plan of goods in a warehouse. Robots follow instructions to collect the goods. What has this robot collected?

b Write instructions for the robot to collect a computer tablet and a games console.

c Write some more orders and the instructions for the robot to follow to pick them.

Robot instructions
Turn left; forward 2, PICK;
turn right; forward 4, PICK;
turn right; forward 2;
turn right; forward 4.

Did you know?

A long time ago, people thought the Earth was flat. They thought you could fall off the edge!

Now we know the Earth is a sphere. You can go all the way around the world on a plane.

Pattern and ordering

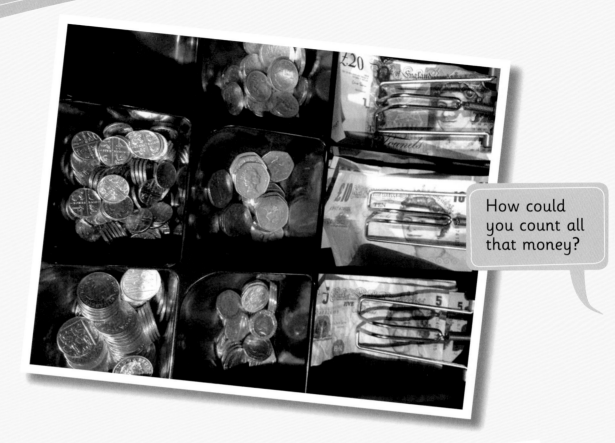

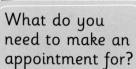
What do you need to make an appointment for?

What patterns can you see?

Have they got the same amount?

Teacher's Guide
Look at the pictures with the children and discuss the questions.
See pages 136–7 of the *Teacher's Guide* for key ideas to draw out.

125

Let's learn

You need:
- place-value cards 4 9
- metre stick
- Base 10 apparatus
- small objects

37 is bigger than 54 because 3 plus 7 is 10 and 5 plus 4 is 9. 10 is more than 9.

No, 54 is bigger than 37 because 54 has 5 tens and 37 only has 3. Check on the number line.

Ordering numbers

A number line shows numbers in order.
This one shows numbers from 0 to 100.

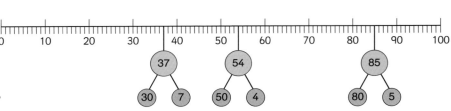

37 is less than 54.   85 is more than 54.

2-digit numbers are made of tens and ones.
Look at how many tens each number has.
You can order numbers from 0 tens to 9 tens.

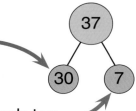

Look at how many ones to order numbers within each ten.

Ordering things

You can order things using these words:

first   second   third   next   last

The **first** bead is yellow.
The **second** bead is red.
The **third** bead is green.
The **next** bead is blue.
The **last** bead is purple.

Teacher's Guide

Before working through the *Textbook*, study page 138 of the *Teacher's Guide* to see how the concepts should be introduced. Read and discuss the page with the children. Provide concrete resources to support exploration.

1

Make and order numbers. Use a set of place-value cards.

Shuffle the tens cards. Place them face down.
Shuffle the ones cards. Place them face down.

Take the top card from each pile.
Make a 2-digit number.
Make 9 numbers.
Order them from smallest to largest.

2

Answer these. Order the numbers from smallest to largest.

a   51, 48, 23, 16, 35

b   67, 25, 86, 63, 58

c   34, 29, 32, 36, 21

d   65, 60, 66, 63, 68

3

Apply. Make a number line from 0 to 100.

Use a metre stick and a long strip of paper to make a number line. Label the tens. Mark these numbers on your number line:

| 84 | 39 | 72 | 53 | 31 | 87 | 75 | 56 |

Check the numbers are in the right place.
Add 4 more numbers.
Check they are in the right place.

4

Think.

Choose 6 objects.
Decide which is first, second, third, fourth, fifth and last.
Give them to your partner.
Tell them how to put them in your order.
Do the same with your partner's objects.

> Have another turn each. Put the objects in a different order.

Teacher's Guide
See page 139 of the *Teacher's Guide* for ideas of how to guide practice.
Work through each step together as a class to develop children's conceptual understanding.

127

Let's learn

5 add 5 is 10. 10 is an even number. When we count in fives, all the numbers are even.

5 is an odd number so only half of them are even: 5, 10, 15, 20, 25, 30, 35, 40, 45, 50. They go odd, even, odd, even ...

Counting in fives

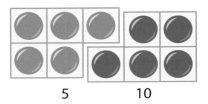

5   10

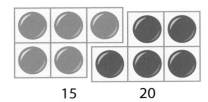

15   20

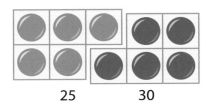

25   30

Look at the number pattern for counting in fives. What do you notice?

Each arrow shows us 5 more.
To find 5 less, go back along an arrow.

What is 5 more than 55?
What is 5 less than 70?

5 more

1	2	3	4	5	6	7	8	9	10
11	12	13	14	15	16	17	18	19	20
21	22	23	24	25	26	27	28	29	30
31	32	33	34	35	36	37	38	39	40
41	42	43	44	45	46	47	48	49	50
51	52	53	54	55	56	57	58	59	60
61	62	63	64	65	66	67	68	69	70
71	72	73	74	75	76	77	78	79	80
81	82	83	84	85	86	87	88	89	90
91	92	93	94	95	96	97	98	99	100

5p coins

  =

   =

       = 50

How many 5p coins do you need to make £1?

1 Answer these. Count in fives.

a How many?

b How many arms on all the starfish?

c How many fingers?

d How much money?

2 Answer these.

Write 5 less than each number.

| 35 | 10 | 55 | 90 | 5 |

Write 5 more than each number.

| 40 | 65 | 15 | 55 | 80 |

3 Apply.

How many 5p coins do you need to pay each price?

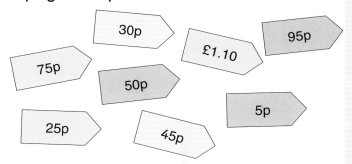

30p

95p

£1.10

75p

50p

5p

25p

45p

Take 13, 5p coins. Which of these prices are you not able to pay?

4 Think.

You have 4 digit cards.

5 2 7 0

How many different numbers can you make that are multiples of 5?

How many numbers can you make that are **not** multiples of 5?

Teacher's Guide See page 141 of the *Teacher's Guide* for ideas of how to guide practice. Work through each step together as a class to develop children's conceptual understanding.

129

Clocks

Let's learn

You need:
- clock with moveable hands
- clock faces

It's 6 past 10.

No, the minute hand has gone halfway around the clock to the 6, so it's half past 10.

Half past

It takes 1 hour for the minute hand to go around the clock.

It takes half an hour for the minute hand to go halfway around.

Halfway from 1 hour to the next is called half past.

Clock fives

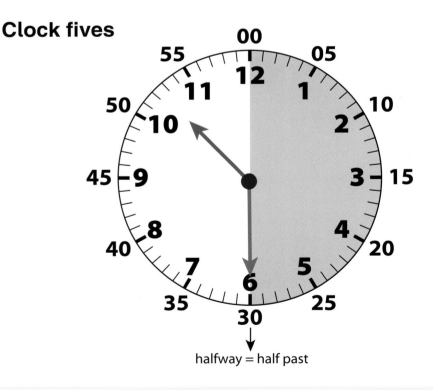

halfway = half past

Half an hour ago, it was 10 o'clock.

In half an hour it will be 11 o'clock.

Teacher's Guide

Before working through the *Textbook*, study page 142 of the *Teacher's Guide* to see how the concepts should be introduced. Read and discuss the page with the children. Provide concrete resources to support exploration.

1 Answer these.

Write ☐ o'clock or half past ☐ for each clock.

a

b

c

d

e

f

g

h

2 Draw.

Draw each time on a clock face.

a half past 10   d half past 6   g half past 5

b half past 8   e half past 2   h half past 12

c 9 o'clock   f 3 o'clock

3 Apply. Show the new time.

a

half an hour later

b

half an hour earlier

c

1 hour later

d

1 hour earlier

4 Think.

Show:
- an earlier time
- a different earlier time
- 2 later times.

Teacher's Guide
See page 143 of the *Teacher's Guide* for ideas of how to guide practice.
Work through each step together as a class to develop children's
conceptual understanding.

131 ★

Repeating patterns

Let's learn

There are always 2 or 3 different shapes in a repeating pattern.

There might be, but the pattern could be just 1 shape in different colours or sizes.

Change the colour

Repeating patterns repeat things in the same order.

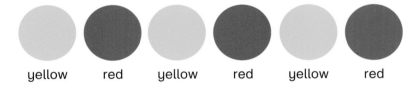

| yellow | red | yellow | red | yellow | red |

What colour will the next circle be?

Change the shape or size

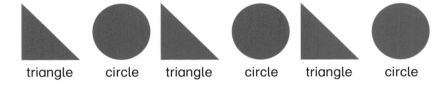

| triangle | circle | triangle | circle | triangle | circle |

Which shape comes next?

| big | small | big | small | big | small | big |

What size will the next elephant be?

Teacher's Guide

Before working through the *Textbook*, study page 144 of the *Teacher's Guide* to see how the concepts should be introduced. Read and discuss the page with the children. Provide concrete resources to support exploration.

1 **What's next?**

Draw the next shape in each pattern.

a

b

c

2 **Find.**

Find the missing shape or picture in each pattern.

a
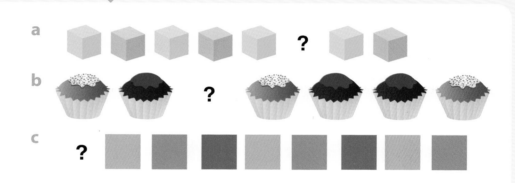

b

c

3 **Draw.**

Copy each pattern with shape tiles.

Each pattern has an extra shape in the wrong place.

Take it out and draw it.

What position was the shape in?

a

b

c

4 **Think.**

Choose 3 different objects or shapes to make a repeating pattern.

Use at least 3 of each.

Take 1 piece away from your pattern. Can your friend say what is missing?

Teacher's Guide

See page 145 of the *Teacher's Guide* for ideas of how to guide practice.
Work through each step together as a class to develop children's
conceptual understanding.

133 ★

Number builder

Let's play

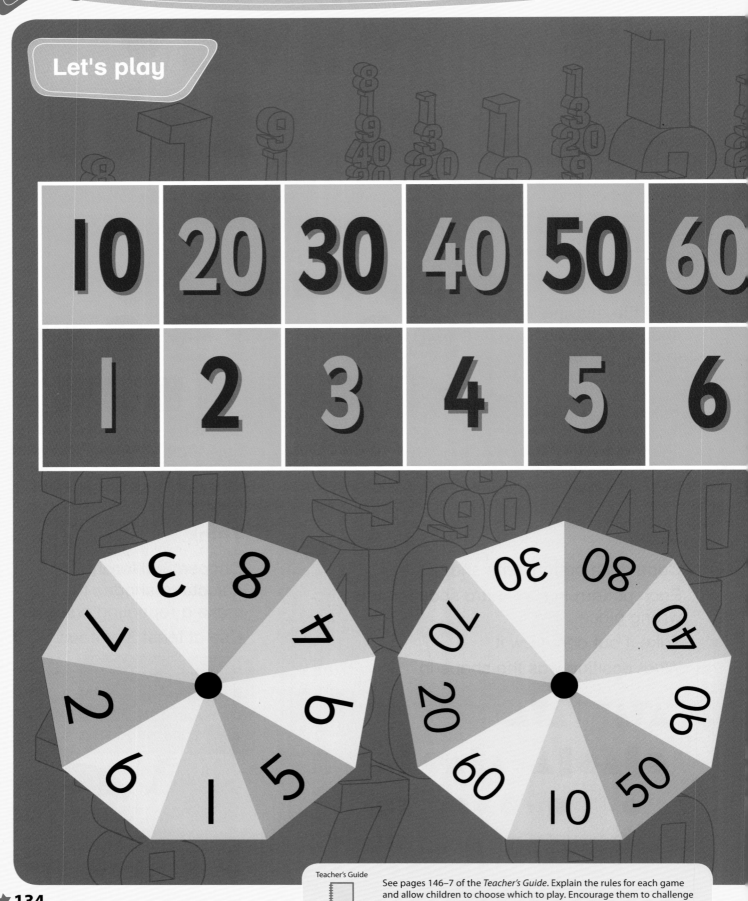

10	20	30	40	50	60
1	2	3	4	5	6

Teacher's Guide

See pages 146–7 of the *Teacher's Guide*. Explain the rules for each game and allow children to choose which to play. Encourage them to challenge themselves and practise what they have learnt in the unit.

1 **Highest, lowest**

Spin to build the highest number you can. Who will get the most counters first?

2 **Closest to 50**

Spin to build a number as close to 50 as you can. Who will get the most counters first?

3 **Your game**

Make up your own game using the gameboard.

135

And finally ...

Let's review

1

You need:
- place-value cards 4 9
- Base 10 apparatus

Who won the race?

Use these clues. The winner's number:

- does not have 2 tens
- does not have 5 tens
- does not have 5 ones

- does not have 1 less than 5 ones
- is even.

Make up some clues to show who came last.

2

Everything in the shop costs £5.

You need:
- 5p and £1 coins 5p £1
- banknotes £5 £10

George spent £40.
How many things did he buy?

Shakira has £15.
How many things can she buy?

Jamie bought:
- a book
- 2 DVDs
- a t-shirt
- a rucksack.

How much did he spend?

Teacher's Guide

See pages 148–9 of the *Teacher's Guide* for guidance on running each task. Observe children to identify those who have mastered concepts and those who require further consolidation.

3

Continue the patterns. What is the 9th and 15th shape in each pattern?

a

b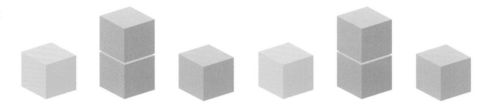

c

Make your own repeating pattern. The 7th shape must be a white square.

Did you know?

Numbers don't really exist, just like dragons! You can have 5 apples but 5 on its own isn't something real.

We have to count things and write numbers to see how they work.

Solving problems

I wonder how many more £1 than £2 coins there are?

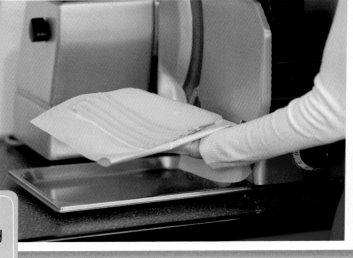

I wonder how many slices they are buying?

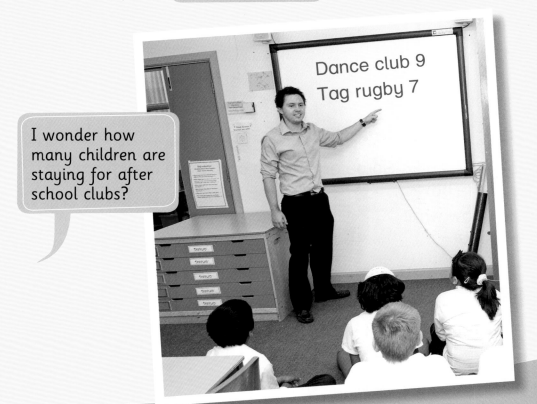

Dance club 9
Tag rugby 7

I wonder how many children are staying for after school clubs?

Teacher's Guide

Look at the pictures with the children and discuss the questions.
See pages 150–1 of the *Teacher's Guide* for key ideas to draw out.

139 ★

You need:
- ten frames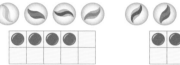
- number lines

Let's learn

I'm going to buy a box of 4 cakes. Some will be strawberry and some vanilla. I wonder what I'll get?

There could be 1 strawberry and 3 vanilla, 2 strawberry and 2 vanilla or 1 vanilla and 3 strawberry. I used my number bonds for 4 to help!

The bar model: whole unknown

Sam has 4 marbles and Jen has 5 marbles. How many marbles do they have altogether?

You could count or draw marbles or circles to find out.

Or you could use the bar model to show what you need to work out.

Use number bonds, doubles, a number line or a ten frame to work out what you don't yet know.

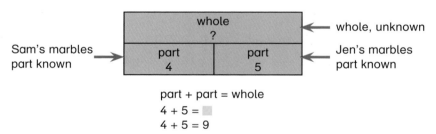

Sam's marbles part known

Jen's marbles part known

whole, unknown

part + part = whole

4 + 5 = ■

4 + 5 = 9

The bar model: 2 parts unknown

There are 6 cakes in a box. Some are vanilla and some are chocolate. What could be in the box?

Drawing bars to show what you need to work out.

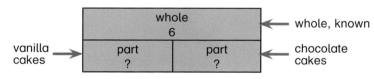

vanilla cakes

chocolate cakes

whole, known

part + part = whole

■ + ■ = 6

There could be:

Vanilla	Chocolate	
5	1	5 + 1
4	2	4 + 2
3	3	3 + 3
2	4	2 + 4
1	5	1 + 5

Teacher's Guide

Before working through the *Textbook*, study page 152 of the *Teacher's Guide* to see how the concepts should be introduced. Read and discuss the page with the children. Provide concrete resources to support exploration.

1 Answer these.

Draw bars to help see what you know and what you do not know.

a   There are 6 boys and 8 girls playing a game. How many children are playing the game altogether?

b   There are 7 toy cars and 5 toy trucks. How many toy vehicles are there altogether?

2 Answer these.

a   There are 7 brown horses and 4 white horses in a field. How many horses are in the field altogether?

b   A farmer has 6 sheep and 7 lambs in a field. How many sheep and lambs are in the field altogether?

c   There are 7 hens and 9 chicks in a farmyard. How many hens and chicks are in the farmyard altogether?

d   A farmer has 8 cows in the barn and 7 in the field. How many cows does he have altogether?

3 Solve.

Ali collects 10p and 5p coins. In a week, he collected 50p. Which coins could he have?

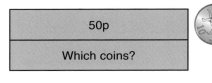

4 Think.

There are 18 flowers in a bunch. Some are red and some are white.

Ann's mum would like 1 or 2 more white flowers than red flowers. How many flowers are red and how many flowers are white in her bunch?

You need:

- ten frames
- number lines

Let's learn

If there are 7 bananas and there are 2 more bananas than apples there must be 9 apples because 7 + 2 is 9.

If there are 2 more bananas than apples, there must be fewer apples than bananas. That means 7 – 2 apples, which is 5 apples. We could draw something to help us understand the problem!

The bar model: 1 part unknown

Mum baked 20 cookies. 12 were chocolate and the rest were lemon. How many lemon cookies were there?

Draw bars to show what you need to work out.

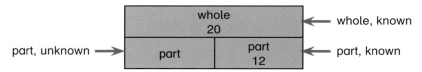

whole, known

part, unknown →

part, known

whole – part = part
20 – 12 = ▨
20 – 12 = 8

Use number bonds, a number line or ten frames to work out what you do not yet know.

Comparison bar model

There are 2 more bananas than apples. If there are 7 bananas, how many apples are there?

difference 2
7 – 2 = 5

You can also show this problem using bars.

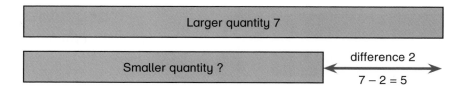

Larger quantity 7

Smaller quantity ?

difference 2
7 – 2 = 5

Teacher's Guide

Before working through the *Textbook*, study page 154 of the *Teacher's Guide* to see how the concepts should be introduced. Read and discuss the page with the children. Provide concrete resources to support exploration.

1 Answer these.

Draw bars to help see what you know and what you do not know.

a   There were 12 cookies on a plate. If 7 cookies were eaten, how many cookies were left?

b   There were 12 eggs in a carton. If 4 were used, how many eggs were left?

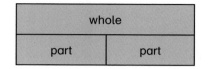

2 Answer these.

a   There are 17 cauliflowers in the vegetable patch. We used 5 to make cauliflower cheese. How many cauliflowers are left in the vegetable patch?

b   15 daffodils were in the garden. Dad picked 8. How many daffodils are left in the garden?

c   We used 9 of today's eggs at breakfast. We collected 14 eggs before breakfast. How many of today's eggs are left?

d   We ate 7 bananas from the bunch of 11 bananas that Mum brought home. How many bananas are left?

3 Solve.

Shakira has saved 2 more 10p coins than 5p coins. If she has saved four 10p coins, how many 5p coins has she saved?

You could arrange your coins in bars to help you.

4 Think.

Tamsin drew these bars to help her solve a problem. What could the problem be?

Larger quantity 19

Smaller quantity 13   difference ?

Teacher's Guide
See page 155 of the *Teacher's Guide* for ideas of how to guide practice. Work through each step together as a class to develop children's conceptual understanding.

143 ★

Calculation hunt

Let's play

Start

0 + 1

16 – 4   6 + 8   19 – 3   13 + 4

17 – 2   19 – 16

7 + 8   2 + 2

18 – 5   20 – 3   1 + 2

6 + 4   8 + 3   8 – 6

19 – 1   4 + 1

5 + 2   13 – 7

15 – 5   13 + 6   7 + 6   15 – 8   20 + 0

Teacher's Guide

See pages 156–7 of the *Teacher's Guide*. Explain the rules for each game and allow children to choose which to play. Encourage them to challenge themselves and practise what they have learnt in the unit.

20 − 0	1 + 1	14 − 0
	12 + 4	17 − 6
17 − 16		12 + 6
		12 − 7
		5 + 4
3 + 3		14 − 5
	17 − 13	6 + 2
20 − 1	11 − 3	12 + 0

You need:
- 1–6 dice
- counters

 Collect 1 to 20
Collect each calculation you land on. Who can collect one for every total from 1 to 20 first?

 Hunt the number
Choose 5 numbers between 1 and 20. Who can find the calculations with the matching totals first?

 Your number game
Make up your own game using the gameboard.

And finally ...

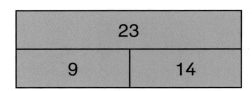

Let's review

Oliver, Jack and their mum have travelled 9 miles of a 14 mile journey to visit Granny and Grandad. Jack wants to know how much further they have to travel.

23	
9	14

$9 + 14 = 23$

Oliver used the bar method to help him work out an answer, but he thinks he has gone wrong somewhere.

Draw the correct bars and use them to find out how much further they have to travel.

Use the bar model to show what you know and what you do not know!

A minibus has 18 seats, including the driver's seat. Mr Smith drives groups of children to the swimming pool and always has 2 other adults in the minibus.

The minibus is full for his first journey of the day. How many boys and how many girls could be on the minibus?

Teacher's Guide

See pages 158–9 of the *Teacher's Guide* for guidance on running each task. Observe children to identify those who have mastered concepts and those who require further consolidation.

When I add 2 numbers together, their sum is 13. What could my numbers be?

13	
?	?

When I subtract my numbers, their difference is 3. What are my numbers?

Did you know?

The Ancient Egyptian sign for addition looked like a pair of legs walking in the same direction as the text was written. For subtraction, the same sign was used but facing the opposite way to the writing.

1 is the number we see more than any other number. If you look at numbers on a page of newspaper, there will be more numbers beginning with 1 than any other number.

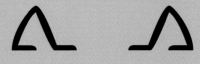

Exploring halves, quarters and arrays

How many hands on 2 children?

If I broke each tower in half, how many cubes would it have?

Where would you cut the red ribbon in half?

How far round has the minute hand moved?

I wonder how many pieces there are.

Teacher's Guide
Look at the pictures with the children and discuss the questions.
See pages 160–1 of the *Teacher's Guide* for key ideas to draw out.

149 ⭐

Let's learn

I want the big half!

'In half' means both parts are the same size.

Halving a quantity

To halve something, it is split into 2 equal parts.

Half of the juice is in each glass.

2 children can take half of these toy cars each.
How many will they get?

Halving a shape

The pizza is cut in half.

The sandwich is cut in half.

Teacher's Guide

Before working through the *Textbook*, study page 162 of the *Teacher's Guide* to see how the concepts should be introduced. Read and discuss the page with the children. Provide concrete resources to support exploration.

1 Count.

How many acrobats altogether?

How many would half be?

a

b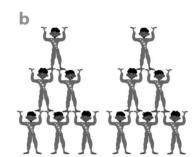

c

2 Answer this.

Which of these is divided into halves?

a

b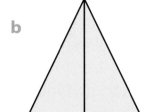

c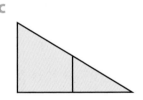

3 Solve.

Which is the other half of:

a The sandwich?

b The ribbon?

1
2
3
4

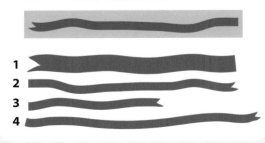

4 Think.

Jen loves chocolate.

Should she choose all of this chocolate bar ...

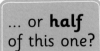

... or **half** of this one?

Why?

Teacher's Guide

See page 163 of the *Teacher's Guide* for ideas of how to guide practice. Work through each step together as a class to develop children's conceptual understanding.

151 ★

13b Quarters

You need:
- interlocking cubes
- money (coins) 2p 10p
- modelling dough
- plastic knife
- buttons or counters

We have shared the pizza between 4. Each person has a quarter.

No. Each of the 4 quarters must be equal – that should be 2 pieces each.

4 equal parts

4 equal parts are called quarters. Each part is 1 quarter.

These shapes have been divided into 4 quarters.
Each part is the same size.

Sharing between 4

To divide something equally between 4 groups –
give 1 quarter of the whole set to each group.

£20 divided between
4 people gives £5 each.
A quarter of £20 equals £5.

Use cubes to help you divide into quarters.

Teacher's Guide

Before working through the *Textbook*, study page 164 of the *Teacher's Guide* to see how the concepts should be introduced. Read and discuss the page with the children. Provide concrete resources to support exploration.

1 **Make.**

Use dough to make models of these cakes.
Cut each cake into quarters.
Draw your cakes.

2 **Look.** Which are not divided into quarters?

a 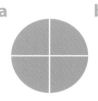 b   c   d

e

3 **Apply.**

Make these towers.
Break them into quarters.
How many cubes
in 1 quarter?

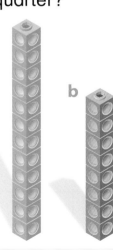

4 **Think.**

Is it true or false?

> I can share any even number of buttons into quarters.

> I can share any odd number of buttons into quarters.

Investigate with buttons.

Teacher's Guide   See page 165 of the *Teacher's Guide* for ideas of how to guide practice.
Work through each step together as a class to develop children's
conceptual understanding.

153

13c Multiplying and dividing

Let's learn

I can count all the rings in the box. 1, 2, 3, 4 …

You can count them quicker in larger numbers – 5, 10, 15, 20, 25. 5 rows of 5 equals 25.

You need:
- egg box
- number track
- number tiles

Arrays

Groups of the same number can be set out in arrays.

Arrays can help to work out problems.

There are 6 eggs.

2 rows of 3 equals 6.

3 rows of 2 equals 6.

Number tracks

We can solve some problems using a number track.

All of the jumps are the same size.

2 jumps of 3 equals 6.

3 jumps of 2 equals 6.

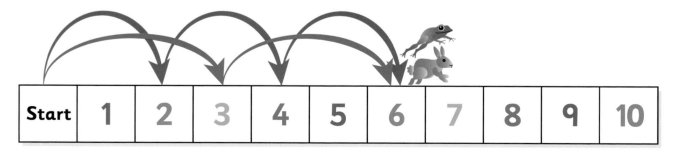

| Start | 1 | 2 | 3 | 4 | 5 | 6 | 7 | 8 | 9 | 10 |

Teacher's Guide

Before working through the *Textbook*, study page 166 of the *Teacher's Guide* to see how the concepts should be introduced. Read and discuss the page with the children. Provide concrete resources to support exploration.

1

Count. How many:

a   carrots?   b   strawberry plants?   c   beetroots?

2

Draw and count.

a   5 rows of cabbages with 4 in each row.
How many cabbages?

b   2 rows of flowers with 9 in each row.
How many flowers?

3

Apply.

Count steps to the house.

a   Baby Bear steps in ones on the stepping stones.

b   Goldilocks steps in twos.

c   Mother Bear steps in fives.

d   Father Bear steps in tens.

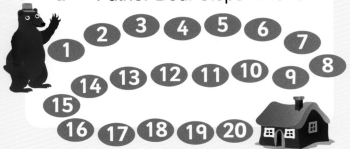

4

Think.

There are 20 stairs to the bedroom.
How many steps does each bear take?

10 stairs at a time

5 stairs at a time

2 stairs at a time

Draw a number track to help you.

Teacher's Guide

See page 167 of the *Teacher's Guide* for ideas of how to guide practice. Work through each step together as a class to develop children's conceptual understanding.

155 ★

Fractions races

Let's play

Start → 1	2	3	4	5 Forward half of 4	6
20 Back quarter of 8	19	18	17	16	15
21	22 Forward half of 10	23	24	25 Back half of 12	26
40 Back quarter of 4	39	38	37 Forward half of 8	36	35
41	42 Forward half of 12	43	44	45	46 Back half of 20

Teacher's Guide

See pages 168–9 of the *Teacher's Guide*. Explain the rules for each game and allow children to choose which to play. Encourage them to challenge themselves and practise what they have learnt in the unit.

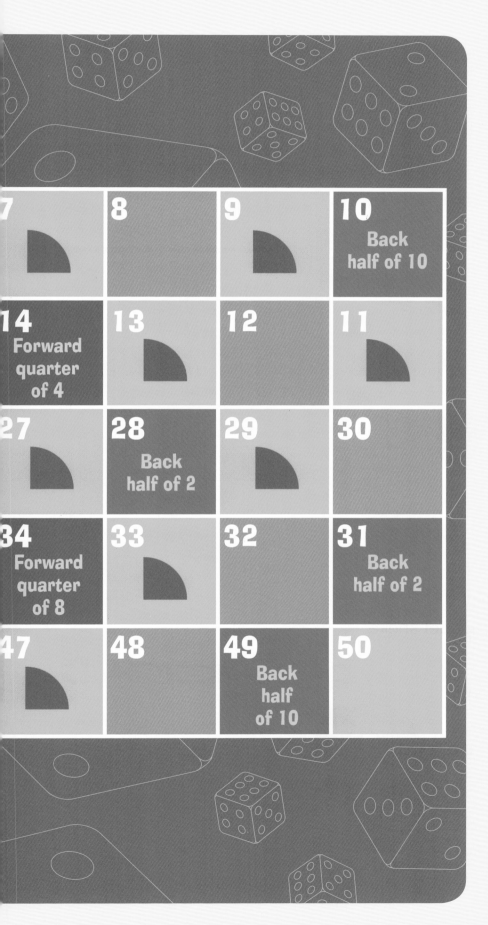

1 **Circles race**

Throw a dice. If you land on a ◣ take one quarter of a circle. Try to reach 50 with the most full circles.

2 **Dice race**

Throw a dice, follow the instructions on the squares, and try to reach 50 first.

3 **Your game**

Design your own game using the gameboard.

And finally ...

Let's review

1

Each of these towers has been broken in half.
How many cubes were in each tower before?

You need:
- interlocking cubes
- paper clips

a    b    c    d

This is Sam's model snake.

Jen's model is half as long.
How many clips does she use?

Teacher's Guide

See pages 170–1of the *Teacher's Guide* for guidance on running each task.
Observe children to identify those who have mastered concepts and those who
require further consolidation.

2 Divide a piece of paper into quarters.

How many quarters are there?
What shape are the quarters?

Sam takes a quarter of the £1 coins out of each bag. How much money does he take from each bag?

You need:
- small bags
- £1 coins

£8   £24   £16

3

How many lambs?

The lamb makes 9 jumps of 2.
Where does he end?
The lamb makes jumps of 5. He lands on 25.
How many jumps?

You need:
- small toy lamb

Did you know?

Is it possible to fold a piece of paper in half more than 7 times?

Yes! In 2012 students folded the length of a roll of toilet paper in half 13 times.

Making turns

What size is each apple?

Where can you go?

Describe going up the staircase.

I wonder where you can go?

Can you divide the clock face into quarters?

Teacher's Guide

Look at the pictures with the children and discuss the questions.
See pages 172–3 of the *Teacher's Guide* for key ideas to draw out.

161 ★

Let's learn

You need:
- 2-D shapes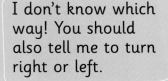
- letter shapes

Make a quarter turn.

I don't know which way! You should also tell me to turn right or left.

Three quarters – $\frac{3}{4}$

This fraction is 3 parts of the 4 equal parts.

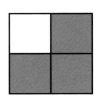

$\frac{3}{4}$ ← The number of pieces we have.

← The total number of pieces altogether.

We read this fraction as 'three quarters'.
Three quarters is equal to 3 lots of 1 quarter.

The red arrow has made $\frac{3}{4}$ of a whole turn.

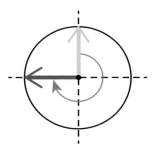

Turning in quarter turns

Look at the cat. It is turning to the right in quarter turns.

$\frac{1}{4}$ turn $\frac{1}{2}$ turn $\frac{3}{4}$ turn   whole turn

↑   →   ↓   ←   ↑

A clock turns in the same way.

Teacher's Guide

Before working through the *Textbook*, study page 174 of the *Teacher's Guide* to see how the concepts should be introduced. Read and discuss the page with the children. Provide concrete resources to support exploration.

1

Draw.

Find a rectangle.
Draw around it.

Turn it right by a quarter. Draw it again.
Repeat until you have turned a complete turn.
Do the same with a triangle.

2

Draw.

Draw each shape. Turn each
3 quarters of a turn to the right.
Draw what they will look like.

a   b   c

3

Apply.

Sam is at
the zoo.

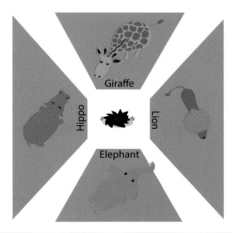

Start with Sam facing the giraffe each
time. What can he see if he turns:

a $\frac{1}{2}$ a turn to the right?

b $\frac{3}{4}$ of a turn to the right?

c $\frac{1}{2}$ a turn to the left?

d $\frac{1}{4}$ of a turn to the right?

e $\frac{1}{4}$ of a turn to the left?

4

Think.

Which capital letters look the same after $\frac{1}{4}$ or $\frac{1}{2}$ of a turn?

Teacher's Guide

See page 175 of the *Teacher's Guide* for ideas of how to guide practice.
Work through each step together as a class to develop children's
conceptual understanding.

163 ★

Programming floor robots

Let's learn

There are 4 sides to a square. To write a program to draw a square I will need 4 commands.

I don't think that's going to work! You need to make a turn after drawing each side.

You need:
- floor robot
- box

Floor robot controls

Go forwards 1 step.

Press GO to run the program.

Make a quarter turn left.

Make a quarter turn right.

Press to clear the memory.

Press to stop for a while. Press again to continue the journey.

Go backwards 1 step.

Writing a program

Here is the program for a square.
The sides of the square are equal to 1 step.

Forward 1, quarter turn right   ↑1, →
Forward 1, quarter turn right   ↑1, →
Forward 1, quarter turn right   ↑1, →
Forward 1   ↑1

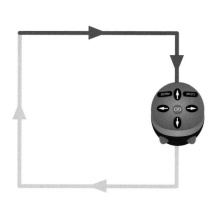

Think about how the robot has moved.

Teacher's Guide

Before working through the *Textbook*, study page 176 of the *Teacher's Guide* to see how the concepts should be introduced. Read and discuss the page with the children. Provide concrete resources to support exploration.

1

Write.

Write a program to draw a square.
Make the sides of the square 3 steps long.

2

Program.

Put a box on the floor.
Program your floor robot to travel around it.

3

Apply.

How far does your floor robot travel in 1 step?
Use a ruler to draw this track.

```
                          3 steps
                   ┌──────────────── Finish
            1 step │
Start ─────────────┘
        3 steps
```

Try the robot on your track.
Draw your own track.

4

Investigate.

1 2 3 4 5 ...

Jen increases the number of steps by 1 after each turn. What happens?

> Forwards 1 step, turn right, forwards 2 steps, turn right ...

Guess the robot's path.
Now test it.

Teacher's Guide

See page 177 of the *Teacher's Guide* for ideas of how to guide practice.
Work through each step together as a class to develop children's
conceptual understanding.

165 ★

Sailing races

Let's play

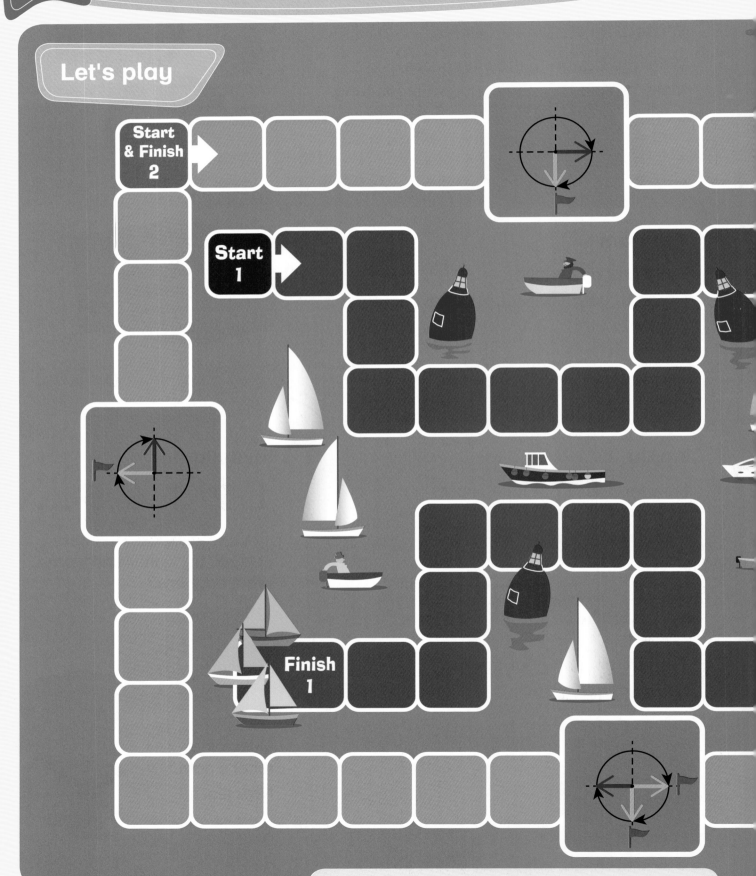

Teacher's Guide

See pages 178–9 of the *Teacher's Guide*. Explain the rules for each game and allow children to choose which to play. Encourage them to challenge themselves and practise what they have learnt in the unit.

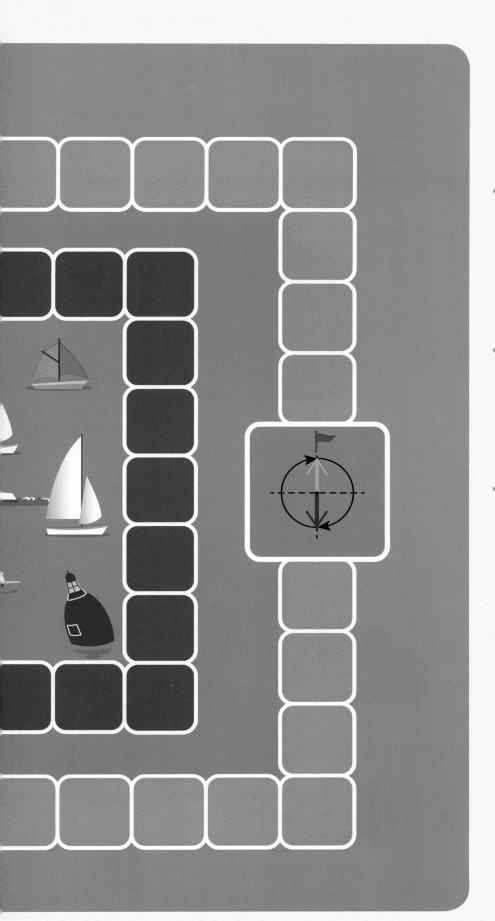

1 **Race around the buoys**

Your counter is your boat. Race around the buoys!

2 **Sail right home**

Make turns to the right to collect the flags.

3 **Your game**

Make up your own game using the gameboard.

And finally ...

Let's review

1

Jen is in the middle of a village. There is a lake, a hill, a castle and a café.

Start with Jen facing the café each time.
This is what she sees when she turns:

- half turn right – she can see the lake
- quarter turn right – she can see the castle
- three-quarter turn right – she can see the hill.

Draw a picture of the village.
Draw Jen in the middle.
Show the positions of the café, lake, castle and hill.

2

a   Forwards 4 steps, backwards 4 steps. Is your floor robot back where it started?

You need:
- floor robot

b   Forwards 4 steps. Oh dear! The backwards button is broken.

How can you move the robot back to where it started?

Teacher's Guide

 See pages 180–1 of the *Teacher's Guide* for guidance on running each task. Observe children to identify those who have mastered concepts and those who require further consolidation.

Look at the numbers.
Choose a number.
Write a program to draw it.

Try another.
Compare your programs with your friend.

Some are easy – others are a bit trickier!

Did you know?

The first programmable floor robots were made about 70 years ago. The first ones used in schools were called Turtles!

They were called Turtles after the Mock Turtle in the story *Alice in Wonderland*.

1 Glossary

2-dimensional (2-D)

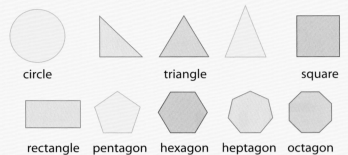

circle   triangle   square

rectangle   pentagon   hexagon   heptagon   octagon

3-dimensional (3-D)

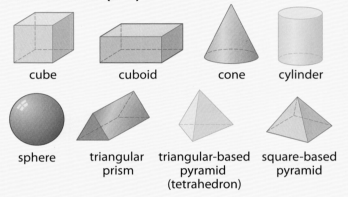

cube   cuboid   cone   cylinder

sphere   triangular prism   triangular-based pyramid (tetrahedron)   square-based pyramid

A

addend

The number being added in an addition calculation.
augend + addend = sum (or total)

$$3 + 5 = 8$$
augend   addend   sum/total

addition

A mathematical operation combining two or more numbers to find a total.
augend + addend = sum (or total).

$$3 + 5 = 8$$
augend   addend   sum/total

array

An arrangement of numbers, shapes or objects in rows of equal size and columns of equal size, used to find out how many altogether.

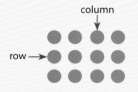
column
row →

augend

The number being added to is in an addition calculation.
augend + addend = sum (or total)

$$3 + 5 = 8$$
augend   addend   sum/total

B

balance

Things are balanced when both sides have equal value,
e.g. $3 + 4 = 2 + 5$ and $1000 g = 1 kg$.

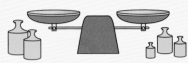

C

calendar

A list of the days of the year, arranged by month, week and day.

capacity

The amount a container holds. It is measured in litres or millilitres, e.g. the capacity of a 2 litre bottle is 2 litres.

centimetre

A unit of length, 1 metre = 100 centimetres. Symbol: cm.

change

The money left over when buying something with a note or coin bigger than the amount needed. The change is given back to the buyer.

circle

A 2-D shape with one curved side and no straight sides.

clock, clock face, hands

A clock is used to show and record time. It can have a circular face with revolving hands to mark hours and minutes, or it can have a digital display.

clockwise, anticlockwise

Clockwise: turning in the same direction as the hands on a clock.

Anticlockwise: turning in the opposite direction to the hands on a clock.

clockwise   anticlockwise

column

A list of numbers, shapes or objects down a page, not across, often in a table or an array.

column

cone

A 3-D shape with a flat, circular face and a curved face. It has one apex (sometimes mistakenly called a vertex) directly above the circular base.

corner

The point on a 2-D shape where two sides meet. Properly called a vertex (plural, vertices).

corner →

cube

A 3-D shape made from six identical squares.

cuboid

A 3-D shape made from six rectangles. Two or four of the rectangles could be squares, e.g. a cereal box. A cube is a special sort of cuboid.

curved

A line that is not straight, e.g. a circle, or a surface that is not flat, e.g. an egg.

cylinder

A 3-D shape with circular ends and one curved face joining the two circular ends.

D

date

How we record the passing of time. Usually given as day of the month, month and then year, e.g. 3rd April 2015.

denominator

The number underneath the line in a fraction.

← numerator
← denominator

difference

How much bigger or smaller one quantity is compared to another. Usually found by subtraction.

The difference between 7 and 5 is 2, 7 – 5 = 2.

digit

The symbols 0, 1, 2, 3, 4, 5, 6, 7, 8 and 9. The value of each digit depends on its position, e.g. in 16, the digit 1 represents one ten while the 6 represents six ones.

division

Sharing or grouping a quantity into equal groups, e.g. 12 ÷ 4 is 12 divided into four parts each of value 3, or 12 shared equally between four people would be 3 each.

double

Two lots of something, multiply by 2.

E

edge

The line made where two faces of a 3-D shape meet. See also *face, vertex*.

equals, equivalent

Symbol: =. Means to have the same value as, e.g. 2 + 4 = 6; 5 + 3 = 7 + 1.

estimate

A sensible guess at how many or how much.

even

A whole number which can be grouped in twos. It is a multiple of 2. See also *odd*.

F

face

A flat surface on a 3-D shape. See also *edge* and *vertex*.

flat

In 2-D and 3-D shapes, not curved.

fraction

Part of a whole.

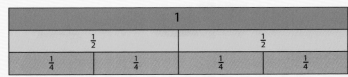

See also *half, quarter*.

G

gram

Symbol: g. A measure of mass or weight. There are 1000 grams in a kilogram. See also *kilogram*.

H

half

When a whole is divided into two equal parts.

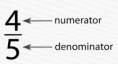

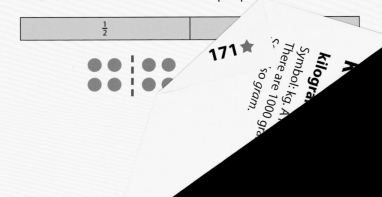

half past

Half an hour has passed since the last o'clock. See also *o'clock*.

halfway between

The middle, between two numbers, e.g. 15 is halfway between 10 and 20.

heavier than, lighter than

Comparing two masses or weights, e.g. 4 kg is heavier than 3 kg, 3 kg is lighter than 4 kg.

heaviest, lightest

Comparing three or more masses or weights, e.g. of 5 kg, 6 kg and 10 kg, 5 kg is the lightest, 10 kg is the heaviest.

heavy, light

Words used to compare mass or weight.

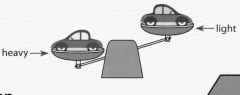

hexagon

A 2-D shape with six straight sides.

hour

Symbol: h. A measure of time. See also *minute* and *second*.

hour hand

The hand on a clock that measures the hours. One complete turn takes 12 hours. See also *minute hand*.

I

inverse

The inverse of add 6 is subtract 6, and the inverse of subtract 6 is add 6. The inverse 'undoes' the action.

m

measure of mass or weight .
ms in a kilogram.

L

length, height

Words used to describe how long or tall something is.

less than

Used when comparing the size of two quantities, e.g. 7 is less than 10. See also *more than*.

litre

Symbol: l . A measure of capacity. 1000 millilitres = 1 litre.

long, longer, longest

Words used when comparing lengths, e.g. a line is 3 cm long, 3 cm is longer than 2 cm. Three lines are 4 cm, 6 cm and 8 cm long. The longest line is 8 cm.

M

mass

Sometimes called weight. How light or heavy something is. Measured in grams and kilograms. See also *gram*, *kilogram*.

measure, measurement

The act of measuring something. We record the measurement with the matching units of measure, e.g. we measure length in metres and capacity in litres.

metre

Symbol: m. A measure of length or height, 100 centimetres = 1 metre.

minuend

The starting number in a subtraction calculation, e.g. 10 (the minuend) – 3 (the subtrahend) = 7 (the difference). See also *subtrahend* and *difference*.

$$10 - 3 = 7 \leftarrow \text{difference}$$

minuend   subtrahend

minute

Symbol: min. A measure of time. See also *second* and *hour*.

minute hand

The hand on a clock face that measures the minutes. One complete revolution takes 60 minutes (one hour). See also *hour hand*.

money

Coins and notes used to buy things with.

more than

Used when comparing the size of two quantities. 10 is more than 7. See also *less than*.

multiple, multiple of

When we start at zero and count in steps of the same size, those numbers are multiples of that step. So 2, 4, 6, 8, 10 and so on are all multiples of 2.

multiply, multiplication

Symbol: ×. Putting groups of the same size together

$2 \times 4 = 2 + 2 + 2 + 2 = 8$

N

number

There are many different types of number, including counting numbers 0, 1, 2, 3 and so on; fractions such as $\frac{1}{4}$, $\frac{1}{2}$; ordinal numbers 1st, 2nd, 3rd and so on.

number bonds/pairs

Pairs of numbers with a particular total, e.g. the number bonds for 10 are all pairs of whole numbers, like 2 and 8, which add up to 10.

number statement

Also called a number sentence, e.g. $4 + 5 = 9$, $8 - 3 = 5$.

numeral

The symbol we write to represent a number. We use the arabic numerals 0, 1, 2, 3, 4, 5, 6, 7, 8 and 9.

numerator

The number above the vinculum. See also *denominator*.

$$\frac{1}{2} \longleftarrow \text{numerator}$$

O

o'clock

A way of describing an exact hour time, e.g. 5 o'clock. The minute hand always point to the 12. See also *half past*.

5 o'clock

odd

A whole number which cannot be put into twos, there will always be one left over. See also *even*.

one less

The number one whole before that number on a number line, e.g. 9 is one less than 10.

one more

The number one whole after that number on a number line, e.g. 9 is one more than 8.

ones

Numbers in the ones place of any number, e.g. 14 is one 10 and 4 ones.

P

parts of a whole

A fraction of a whole number or object. If there are four equal parts of a whole then each part is $\frac{1}{4}$.

pattern

A regular arrangement of shapes or numbers that follows a rule.

pentagon

A 2-D shape with five straight sides.

place, place value

The position of a digit in a number gives its size, e.g. in 23 the digit 2 means 20, but in 12 it means 2.

pyramid, square-based

A 3-D shape with a square base and four triangular faces.

square-based pyramid

Q

quarter

When a whole is divided into four equal parts.

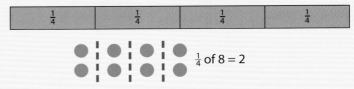

$\frac{1}{4}$ of 8 = 2

R

rectangle

A 2-D shape with four straight sides. A square is a special sort of rectangle four sides the same length.

173 ★

row

A list of numbers, shape across a page, not dow table or an array. See a

S

scales

A way of measuring using a line with equal marks and spaces. This can be a straight line like on a ruler or a curved line like on kitchen scales.

second

Symbol: s. A measure of time.

shape

A 2-D or 3-D object.

sharing

Putting objects into equal-sized groups, 1 at a time, e.g. 10 ÷ 2 = 5 is 10 shared between 2, giving 5 each. See also *fraction*.

short, shorter, shortest

Words used when comparing lengths and heights, e.g. a line is 3 cm long, 2 cm is shorter than 3 cm, three lines are 4 cm, 6 cm and 8 cm long. The shortest line is 4 cm.

side

On a 2-D shape, e.g. a triangle has three sides, a rectangle has 4. See also *corner*.

sphere

A 3-D shape like a ball.

square

A special rectangle where all the sides are the same length. A regular 4-sided shape.

straight line

A straight line has no curves or corners.
␣␣n be drawn using a ruler. See also *curved*.

␣␣tion calculation.

subtraction

A subtraction finds the difference between two numbers. Also called taking away, e.g. 10 (the minuend) – 3 (the subtrahend) = 7 (the difference). See also *minuend*.

$$10 - 3 = 7 \longleftarrow \text{difference}$$

minuend   subtrahend

subtrahend

The number that is subtracted from the minuend, e.g. 10 (the minuend) – 3 (the subtrahend) = 7 (the difference).

$$10 - 3 = 7 \longleftarrow \text{difference}$$

minuend   subtrahend

sum

An addition of two or more numbers or the result of an addition, e.g. augend + addend = sum (or total).

$$3 + 5 = 8$$

augend addend sum/total

T

take away

Another name for subtraction. See also *subtraction*.

tall, taller, tallest

Words used when comparing two or more heights, e.g. Amy is taller than Lili, but Theo is the tallest.

ten less

The number ten before that number on a number line or 100 square, e.g. 40 is ten less than 50.

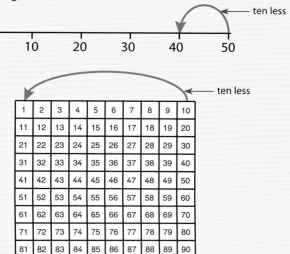

ten more

The number ten after that number on a number line or 100 square, e.g. 50 is ten more than 40.

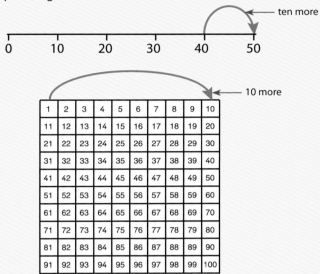

total

Another word for sum, the result of an addition.

triangle

A 2-D shape with three straight sides.

turn (whole turn, half turn, quarter turn, three-quarter turn)

Move like the hands on a clock travel around the clock face. Can be in the same direction as a clock (clockwise) or the opposite direction (anticlockwise).

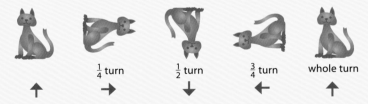

$\frac{1}{4}$ turn $\frac{1}{2}$ turn $\frac{3}{4}$ turn   whole turn

U

units

The standard measures, e.g. the units of length are metres, centimetres.

V

vertex, vertices

The point where two sides meet on a 2-D shape and where three or more faces meet on a 3-D shape.

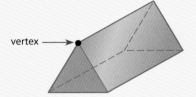

vinculum

$\frac{1}{2}$ ← vinculum

volume

The amount of liquid in a container, e.g. 1 litre of water in a 2 litre bottle. Measured in millilitres and litres. See also *capacity*.